On Retreat

On Retreat

A Lenten Journey

Andrew Walker

continuum

Continuum International Publishing Group
The Tower Building   80 Maiden Lane
11 York Road   Suite 704
London   New York
SE1 7NX   NY 10038

www.continuumbooks.com

The Contemplations were originally composed for the Paternoster Project based at the St Paul's Institute and are used with permission. Some parts of the passages on retreats, spiritual direction and the Examen have appeared previously in *The Tablet* and *The Way*.

First published 2012

British Library Cataloguing-in-Publication Data
A catalogue record for this book is available from the British Library.

ISBN: 978-0-8264-3169-1

Typeset by Fakenham Prepress Solutions, Fakenham, Norfolk NR21 8NN
Printed and bound in India

For Arthur and Elizabeth, my parents in faith, and to Joyce, Jerry, Cecilia and Liz – retreat givers over the years who helped God change my life.

Contents

Introduction

Introducing the journey

Time away for a retreat, while often invaluable, can sometimes seem out of our reach, whether practically, financially or for whatever reason. Sometimes indeed time away and time out seem least possible at those points when we most need the space and freedom they ideally offer. Partly for this reason, the retreat journey offered here is one that can be undertaken at home, in and around daily tasks and work commitments, and in a format that hopefully is flexible enough, and sufficiently adaptable, to offer maximum benefit to any who feel such a journey might be for them at this juncture. A retreat is particularly appropriate during Lent since the seasons of Lent and Easter provide us with the two main models of Christian retreat: the time spent by Jesus alone in the desert, and the time spent together by the first disciples in the upper room, while they awaited the coming of the Holy Spirit.

Most of the changes, developments and unfolding experiences of our faith journey are brought into sharper clarity in times of retreat. This may of course mean that any periods of silence, quiet days or occasions such as this are approached with ambivalence. It's no surprise that we can sometimes be fearful of what God might ask if ever he were given a chance to get a word in; indeed, perhaps it would be worrying if we weren't fearful at all.

We can often resist at first, but faced with the generosity and steadfast love of God we can come to realize that we have a choice and that we may be willing to change our behaviour in the light of this insight. This won't be easy but is certainly possible harnessed to a prayer for greater freedom, and to the desire to want what God might want more than any particular attachment of our own. Our habits so shape our lives and often come to be so much a part of our identity that we can be reluctant to face the fact that they may arise from outmoded patterns of behaviour that have had their day, that there may well be waiting in the wings an invitation from God to grow and to change.

For often, deeper insights are permitted in times of retreat into who we see ourselves to be and how we encounter God, and what those two experiences have to say to each other. It's part indeed of the process of religious formation. Now I'd see religious formation as a becoming over time, indeed a lifetime: a becoming that is a result of the discovery of the Christ in each one of us and of each one of us in Christ. Only the work of the Spirit makes this possible and the job of times of retreat is to facilitate that specific work of the Spirit.

What this will look like will be different for all of us, for our personal story, our temperament, our circumstances will all play their part in what is possible and what is appropriate in growth in faith and increased sensitivity to the ways of our God. But times of retreat are likely to include the more profound elements of opening, widening, deepening and integrating – our desire for God, our ability to experience and respond to his love, our humility and our capacity to be generous in return. And I very much hope that these will be present in your experience of this Lent, facilitated in some way perhaps by this book and the journey, with its various ingredients, that I am proposing. Ultimately the encounter we are looking for is of course a renewed encounter with God, and God after all seems usually remarkably sensitive and generous in using what he is given and in judging what he will ask and invite of us next.

*

Each of the following chapters covers roughly a week or phase of Lent. Each contains three ingredients:

First it includes a narrative of my own experience on the journey as it unfolds, sharing a mixture of my responses to the scripture used, the prayer experienced and the thoughts and feelings that arose. This is certainly not meant to prescribe or even shape your own prayer; I am simply suggesting that this could help to illustrate and orient the week ahead. This subjective account ends with a prayer, different each week, that either I composed myself or found particularly meaningful at that point. Perhaps you might consider composing your own prayers at certain points, or look out for one that works for you that week, using it at the end of your prayer time each day, before allowing another to take its place as the journey moves on.

Then the second section focuses on the opportunities for your own personal prayer. It begins with planning, looking at the possibilities for your own prayer time in the week ahead. Part of starting each week will be to decide not only the content and approach that is going to be right for you but also the times and length of prayer that are going to be possible and appropriate in the week ahead. Scripture texts are then suggested for your prayer: passages for meditation (which you will find in full in the appendix) and some Gospel contemplations written out for use imaginatively if that is helpful. As I see it, the two most useful ways of engaging with Scripture on a retreat journey such as this involve either meditation or contemplation.

Meditation mulls over the Scripture text, reading slowly and prayerfully, stopping where a word or phrase stands out, letting connections be made, thoughts or feeling arise, and allowing an expression of all this to be made to the God in whose presence you have placed yourself.

Contemplation on the other hand invites you to use your imagination to enter the Scriptural story yourself – placing yourself in the scene, making it real and present, so that a first-hand encounter with the Jesus of the Gospel can happen. I have written these out to assist you, some fairly extensively, some more sketchily, but maybe you have your own way of praying this kind of prayer, in which case do stay faithful to that. Neither, anyway, is prescribed – you must decide what and how much and when, so feel free to dispense with any suggestions I might be making, not to use any scripture passage that seems unhelpful, and to judge the pattern of prayer that is going to be right for you. Above all don't commit yourself to too much, especially at first. Better to choose to pray for ten minutes a day and extend that later if you want to do so than to get carried away now and commit to an hour only to have to give it up in due course. The prayer material which is proposed forms the substantial part of the days following, the heart of the week and of the prayer journey.

The third and final ingredient is some concluding reflections which sometimes tease out an aspect of the prayer, at other times an aspect of the spiritual journey. They may not always occur at the right time for you but they are easy to skip over, return to or ignore. This final, more objective, ingredient also suggests that the last phase and day of the week is a reflective or ruminative phase, mulling over what has struck you, turning over relevant thoughts, maybe even making some concluding notes for yourself, recording any observations or insights that have particularly arisen.

Introducing ourselves

Now I'd like to turn from the possible experience ahead to ourselves, those of us beginning the journey; for Lent anyway gives us a chance each year to look afresh at who and where we are in our life before God in the present. It is a chance to take stock, if you like, but also sometimes to venture something new. The journey I am proposing is therefore one that will involve some experimentation and some decision-making on your part: experiments in different ways of praying, some familiar perhaps while others less so, and decisions about what to try out, when to try them out and perhaps how to follow them up. Christian spirituality has many aspects, and different insights have been fostered within different traditions. We will draw on some of these different riches as we journey on, as all of them, I believe, have something to offer us at different stages of our pilgrimage. And I thought to begin by introducing myself, or at least something of my spiritual journey. After all, if you are trusting me to be a companion or guide on your journey through this Lent, you should have some knowledge of the person involved.

My first faith or spiritual experience was largely Franciscan, through my parents who were tertiary or lay Franciscans. This is a spirituality rooted in seeing the Jesus of the Gospel as normative for Christian living. There seems a gentle stress on the rhythm of attendance at the Eucharist and on the life and support of the community, be that family, the third order, the church community or wider society. The notion too of compassion for all things plays its part. This is often seen simply as a fondness for animals and birds but of course it goes much deeper and more widely than that. Francis' first hagiographer, Thomas of Celano, writing in 1229, describes the process of 'contemplating in creatures the wisdom, power and goodness of the Creator.' The created world here is not so much a fallen world but one where one can catch glimpses of a place already experiencing reconciliation. Mission therefore too is present, though not the mission of conversion, but rather of making that inherent reconciliation explicit through relationships of dignity and respect and attitudes of peace and justice. The Franciscan way offered me a sense of celebration of and engagement with the world, and it showed me that faith could be spontaneous and human, informal as well as profound.

Later my journey towards ordination via a school chaplain or two, a retired priest and then theological college was witness to a more Benedictine approach. In contrast this spirituality articulates the aspects of discipline, order and commitment that are needed to foster the awe, humility, realism and joy that are a natural fruit of an encounter with God. Central to the understanding of Benedictine spirituality is its central focus on the monastic life, its stress on obedience and on the rhythms of prayer, *lectio divina* and work in a pattern of daily living. The rhythm of the offices and the stress on community all assisted me here immeasurably and the encounter with the Benedictine spirit brought me a much needed sense of balance and of the discipline of community; it offered me insight into the qualities of proportion and right relationship.

At the age of thirty I came to Ignatius and the Spiritual Exercises. In part the focus of Ignatius on the centrality of the person of Jesus and on the process of the order and rhythm of prayer in his Spiritual Exercises acted as something of a synthesis for what had gone before. But his insight into the role of human frailties and attachments in the process of transformation and greater commitment to Christ was to me immensely liberating. His spirituality is also immensely Trinitarian – a theological doctrine that all too often remains at only a theoretical level for many of us in the church. Ignatius also picks up on the theme and experience of Christian joy but unites it with an experience and expression of love that makes no differentiation between love of God, of neighbour and of the world. The Ignatian approach, with its interplay of rigour and adaptability, showing how one could be Christ-centred and appropriately true to oneself gave me a glimpse of how I really might be an apostle (albeit of a limited sort!) in my life as I experienced it.

The last ten years have brought me to something a bit more composite or perhaps, on reflection, Carmelite. For the Carmelite approach, while it recognizes the value and place of both pastoral outreach and of interior discipline, sees it all within a contemplative approach to all of life. Carmelite spirituality balances creatively both individual solitude and of living in relation to others, both realism about the human condition and insight and humour about the divine initiative in the light of that.

But though this might seem too much of a linear account I don't by any means want to suggest a hierarchy, that one way is somehow superior or more advanced than another. As life and faith evolve, who can tell where the Spirit might lead, and I remain indebted to every aspect of the Christian mystery I have encountered so far.

But what of you? I have started the introductions; how might you continue? or respond? What could you tell of your spiritual path, how might you articulate the stages your faith has been through? One way if you are willing is to take some time to write an account, much as I have done. If that sort of writing seems too intimidating or time-consuming, how about instead reflecting on the following questions?

When did you first learn about prayer?
Who taught you?
How did your prayer evolve or change after that?
What were the significant highs and lows, times of ease and times of difficulty?
How do you experience prayer now?
What do you like about it?
Is there anything ideally you might like to be different?

And now to the possibilities of times of prayer in the days ahead. The pattern below will be that of the weeks ahead. An example is given in the narrative of my own experience, followed by suggested possibilities of meditation or contemplation and concluding with some more general thoughts, here on prayer and spirituality.

Ash Wednesday
Re-encountering God

Narrative

As I begin to think about the coming weeks and my chosen time of retreat my first thought is to ask myself how are we here again at Lent so quickly? Where has the time gone and, worse, what has been achieved? In the light of this two things propose themselves and are suggested.

The first is to honour the year and all that has happened. Immediately I find I start to criticize myself for my selfishness: for doing so much in the year not so much for the glory of God but because of my own temperament and preferences. Even the good things seem in retrospect to arise from choosing to do the things I enjoy or excel in. But this is an exercise in honouring the year not picking holes in it, so I haul myself back and try only to give thanks for it all. If I am good at something, then that is gift, God-given, and I shouldn't be ashamed of exercising it, even at times maximizing it. Even the mistakes and disasters didn't necessarily arise through evil but from either a misunderstanding or a misuse of gifts. Thanks be to God anyway for all the people who have come into my life this year – and those who have left it. I list them in as far as my memory allows and then I commend myself and them all to Him.

The second is to make myself more conscious of what I receive through my senses, to engage them particularly. Thinking can only get you so far in the adventure of faith and indeed thinking can anyway take you away from God's presence. Perhaps God may come first to me through the five senses? I mull on these particularly when I next go out for a walk......

Smell, never my strongest point I believe: some faint wood smoke on the damp air as I sit briefly on the garden bench and the traces of soap from washing my hands earlier stand out. Taste: the soup at lunch and the chutney I smeared on an end of cheese, a musty warm taste when I awake from an after-lunch nap, the pungent, hot taste of the tea that revived me. Sound: rooks in the distance, a squelch of gumboots in mud, the crackle of drifting leaves. Sight: the outline of hills and houses, lowering clouds and a sliver of light as horizon meets horizon – the landscape that is so often just the 'wallpaper' of my living. Touch: my gloves deaden all feeling and maybe that's a parable for my life overall?

I go to church and slip in at the back as a communion service begins. A host of things annoy and distract me: page numbers being announced at every point; endless, wordy intercessions; the modern version of the Lord's Prayer; I could go on. It takes me time to realize that it is not the words or externals that matter but what lies behind them – the heart not the head, perhaps, the trap I often fall into. So what is important here and now is my unfolding relationship with God and so to choose to focus on whatever fruit I can usefully draw from this, as indeed any, experience – the rest is only distraction and certainly here the detail is neither my concern nor my problem.

Prayer

Direct, O Lord, and guide and influence
All that is happening in my mind and heart
During these times of prayer.......

All my thinking and longing and fearing;
My moods and feelings
And ever changing attitudes;

My rememberings and hopes and desires,
My repugnances and resistancies;
My sense of depression or boredom, of joy or hopelessness.

Direct and influence all this
To your great service
And to my growth in the Spirit.   (Sr Elizabeth Smyth)

Planning & Possibilities

Well, this first phase of our journey, these few days between Ash Wednesday and next Sunday are a chance to experiment, try some things out, get a few things wrong. The range of possibilities I want to suggest are choosing one passage from the two below for a time of meditation and/or one of the Gospel passages below that for a period of contemplation.

With meditation I'd suggest reading each passage slowly through, ideally either out loud or in a whisper, letting yourself hear as well as read. Stay with those words that especially draw your attention; repeat any words or phrases that have especial meaning or significance, being aware of any associated feelings. You could even treat the passage as a communication from a dear and much valued friend – to be read and re-read, cherished and pondered on. At the end make any brief notes for yourself that seem useful, especially noting any particular highs or lows; that is to say difficulties or sticky patches, moments when you got distracted or bored, are as much worth noting as any graced moments or particular insights.

Contemplation, as I am using the term here, invites you to participate in the scene, using your imagination to enact it around you as if it were unfolding in the present moment, using all your senses. So this time you should read the passage through to familiarize yourself with it and then imagine yourself present in the scene, watching what happens and listening to what is said, perhaps finding yourself as an observer or assuming the role of one of the participants. I have written these out to help with this but there's no need to use that part of the text; or use it as a springboard – begin by using it and then let the scene and story unfold in its own way. Ultimately all ways of praying involve some sort of encounter with God, some sort of communication. In using the imagination in contemplation we look to foster an encounter with God in Christ where you can see, hear, speak and listen to him. In meditation the word rather than the imagination is the medium for encounter. Neither way, nor indeed any other, is inherently better. But both could be usefully tried out, experimented with, adapted and reflected on......

Whatever form of prayer is being used the way of beginning and ending seems to me important. Above all, that it is something respectful and considered, so perhaps spend just a few minutes each side acknowledging to yourself what it is you are about and ultimately desire. Ask if there is anything that needs to be said or heard – to or from yourself or God. Maybe a repetition of a formal prayer like the 'Our Father' will be the best way to start or close the time, maybe the lighting and extinguishing of a candle. And if there's time perhaps jot down a few brief notes for yourself about what you are doing and how it is going.

Other additional possibilities for these opening days of Lent are a review of the year past – say since last Lent – as I was recommended and recount above, thus to acknowledge and honour all that happened; and/or try a day or period of time where you focus prayerfully on what your senses register and what you receive through them by way of sensation and information. 'Awareness precedes choice' one Jesuit writer once commented – so we begin to ask what is it that we are or can be aware of, both through our senses, our bodies, and through a reflection on recent and not so recent events.

For I see these first few days as a time of orientation and taking stock, and of trying out a committed time of prayer, to see what will be possible and most fruitful in the days ahead. Maybe you will want and be able to commit a set period of time to prayer each day this Lent – and that could be twenty minutes or half an hour or even, for some, an hour. Maybe you will have a space at home and in the day for this kind of prayer and maybe you will be committing a part of your commute or existing pattern of life to it. A lot can be done on a regular bus or tube journey where you can withdraw your attention from your surroundings for a reasonable period and be sure of not missing your stop. Either way do remember quantity doesn't equal quality and the Holy Spirit will use whatever God is offered! How about jotting down some initial thoughts of what pattern of prayer might work for you. What time of day will be best? What length of time possible? What location desirable?

Scripture

Suggested for meditation:

Psalm 104, Philippians 3.7-14

These and all the passages of Scripture for meditation are printed out in full in the Appendix at the end of the book.

Suggested for contemplation:

1. Matthew 5.1-8 The Beatitudes

Seeing the crowds, Jesus went up the hill. There he sat down and was joined by his disciples. Then he began to speak. This is what he taught them:

How happy are the poor in spirit;
theirs is the kingdom of heaven.
Happy the gentle;
they shall have the earth for their heritage.
Happy those who mourn;
they shall be comforted.
Happy those who hunger and thirst for what is right;

they shall be satisfied.
Happy the merciful;
they shall have mercy shown them.
Happy the pure in heart:
they shall see God.

You find yourself in a large, outdoor area, with fine views, maybe familiar to you, maybe not. A large crowd of people are present. It is a warm and sunny day and the crowd is good-humoured. A little way off you see Jesus talking to his disciples. . . . . . . He makes the decision to address the crowd, so he goes a little bit further up the hill, where he can sit and see and be seen by everyone. His disciples go with him. Do you go with them, or do you stay with the crowd? . . . . Perhaps you settle down to listen . . . . . Perhaps you choose to remain standing . . . . . Jesus begins to speak: 'How happy are the poor in spirit; theirs is the kingdom of heaven. Happy the gentle; they shall have the earth for their heritage. Happy those who mourn; they shall be comforted.'

As Jesus speaks, so he looks around, sometimes smiling and nodding in recognition, sometimes making eye contact, sometimes looking with compassion. Perhaps he looks at you . . . . and perhaps you make eye contact . . . . . What is the expression on his face? . . . . Jesus continues, 'Happy those who hunger and thirst for what is right; they shall be satisfied. Happy the merciful; they shall have mercy shown them. Happy the pure in heart; they shall see God.' Jesus stops for a moment. Is there a sign, a touch or a word to be offered or received? . . . . . What is it like for you to be present on this occasion? . . . . . What particularly strikes you and what will you carry away? . . . . . . In a moment Jesus will carry on speaking to the crowds, but see if there is anything finally that needs to be said or done before you prepare to slip away . . . . . . Or maybe you choose to settle back down and to wait for what will be said next. . . . . . In due course bring your awareness of this encounter to a close, slowly bring your consciousness back to the present, knowing of course you can always return at any time if you wish.

2. Mark 2.15-17 Levi's house

While Jesus was having dinner at Levi's house, many tax collectors and sinners were eating with him and his disciples, for there were many who followed him. When the teachers of the law who were Pharisees saw him eating with the sinners and tax collectors, they asked his disciples: 'Why does he eat with tax collectors and sinners?' On hearing this, Jesus said to them, 'It is not the healthy who need a doctor, but the sick. I have not come to call the righteous, but sinners.'

The scene is a large dinner party at the house of someone called Levi. Jesus is there with a number of disciples, with you, and also a large number of people you know might not normally be considered suitable guests. In scriptural language these are the tax collectors and sinners. You find yourself looking around: what sort of people does this actually mean for you? Which are the groups of people you find difficult, or whose behaviour you deem unaccept-able? Who are the people that our society today shuns? And who particularly might you be uncomfortable to find yourself sitting near? And what does that make you feel and think of what Jesus is about? Perhaps you are even annoyed that he seems so indiscriminate?

And you become aware as you look around of a small group of people who enter and ask one or two of the disciples sitting near Jesus, 'Why does put up with this, why is he spending time with these people?' Maybe you add your voice to theirs, or ask a similar question. Jesus replies, 'It is not the healthy who need a doctor, but the sick. I have not come to call the righteous, but sinners.' How do those people look in reaction to that? Maybe Jesus turns and looks at you. How does he look, what might he want to communicate?

Some thoughts on... Prayer and Spirituality

An understanding of the word spirituality is, like it or not, going to undergird our prayer. It is after all a word of mixed parentage with one exasperated writer claiming that current spirituality is like a shanty town with all its consequent lack of norms, history and order.

To address the situation most clearly we could suggest that on the one hand we have what has been called a Greek understanding of the word and on the other an understanding derived from Hebrew thought. On the Greek side of things, 'spirituality' largely covers the aspect of the non-material world – you have matter and you have spirit, a material world and a spiritual world. It is a definition that brings clarity and simplicity to the concept but also has the tendency to wander into the dualism the Christian church is always lurching towards. For if it is clear we live in a world divided between body and soul, faith and life, mind and spirit, church and state, prayer will tend to be aimed at addressing the one rather than the other, the spiritual rather than the material. Prayer then addresses on the whole only one aspect or compartment of life.

On the other hand lies a more Hebraic understanding of the word 'spirituality' that is best summed up in St Paul's words, that it is everything in life lived according to the Spirit of God. This is less clear, of course, but more comprehensive, for there is no rigid demarcation between this world and the things of the Spirit. Here prayer will be of relevance to a much broader realm – work, relationships, the past, fears and desires – as all carry the potential for divine revelation and inspiration.

I suspect it's probably fair to say that for much of Christian history the former view has been the dominant model for understanding spirituality, but that in the last 50 years the latter has greatly overtaken it, partly under the influence of modern listening therapies and partly under the influence of the emerging (or re-emerging) Creation theologies.

One could here reflect on what has been lost in this shift of understanding and practice. But perhaps it is enough for now simply to note the change, that much of the energy around the new is perhaps engendered by its being different from the old, rather than deriving from any inherent superiority, and that already changes are afoot that indicate that what might appear to be a revolution is to be followed by a time of evolution and that current understanding will change and modulate, perhaps incorporating the good and right aspects of what went before while not relinquishing the specific insights and giftedness of what has come after.

What however may be common to these different views, though not perhaps universally so, is the perception of spirituality and prayer as a process of becoming, though the language used will vary from the scriptural at one end of the spectrum (e.g. putting on the mind of Christ) to the therapeutic at the other (e.g. stepping into all I have the potential to be).

The ingredients in this process will vary in importance and timing but will comprise:

- an acknowledgement of the role and work of the Holy Spirit of God
- a recognition of where and how the Holy Spirit is presently most at work be that:
    a call to conversion or repentance in some area of life
    a greater grounding in the majesty and beauty of God
    exploring the adventure of a fuller relationship with Jesus
    responding to a specific call to choice or action
    enduring a time of darkness or suffering
- exploring the fresh possibilities for service in the experience of resurrection joy.

But that's the big picture. What difference might this all make when we actually settle down and commit to some sort of pattern of prayer for the season ahead? I'd suggest thinking of prayer as always needing a beginning, a middle and an end. The beginning and end are mainly your responsibility – the middle, or substance of it, is going to be down to God.

So **beginning**: as you arrive and settle down, ask how you are feeling and what you are bringing. Some things may need to be put aside for the time of prayer, to be collected later, other things may need to be handed over to God for him to look after. Either way your life and all that is going on in it will affect your mood and affect how you are at the start. So what do you need to ask the Lord for at the outset? Then make yourself comfortable, in a place and position where you can be relaxed but focused, attentive and still. Maybe you want to make a slow sign of the Cross, or light a candle. Perhaps pray for the gift of the Holy Spirit, or that God will receive the offering of this time.

And **middle**. This might be a prayer exercise, meditation, contemplation, journalling, whatever you have decided. This will comprise the content of the prayer time and be largely what occupies, at the start at least, your attention. But beyond and behind this content, permitted by the very fact that it distracts and occupies your attention, an unfolding process permitted by the grace of God allows the heart of the prayer to unfold within. What we might call movements of the Spirit, and occasionally their interaction with any countermovements within, reveal the graced presence of God – drawing us closer to his will and the deeper experience of his love.

Finally **end**. As the time draws to a close we need to take control again. Review the time, perhaps jot down a few notes. What was easy, what difficult? What was fruitful, what dry or meaningless? What could we take away by way of insight or what fruit have we garnered? Is there anything in the daily life that faces you that could usefully now be linked to anything that has happened? Perhaps you will want to end with a formal prayer like the Our Father or simply the Glory Be. And then leave the place of prayer, reminding yourself of when you next hope to return. You may be leaving the place of prayer, but you are not leaving God's presence, of course, nor is God leaving your side.

Chapter 1

Lent 1 Discovering myself

Narrative

I get distracted from composing a suggested brief autobiography by turning to think of houses – I have always been keen on architecture, and often when I walk spend my time focusing on the buildings around me. Now I find myself mulling over houses I have lived in, houses I have paid to visit, houses of friends I have shuddered at or been enthused by. If I were to see myself as a house it could be one with immaculate interiors: beautiful rooms, beautifully furnished, beautifully clean and beautifully tidy. A marvellous place to live in style for a short time – but the state of the foundations, the condition of the roof or the unknown absence of a damp-proof course would in the end spoil the whole. And never a place really for relaxation, children or pets; and as for the locked rooms.....

Yet a part of me looks for a different kind of house. A place of comfort not perfect beauty; of character not superficial style; a place that welcomes anybody and everybody, not a place that stops them short to impress or overwhelm. A place so solid that it can absorb or transcend great pain and great joy.

A review of my life follows, falling into sections. The first phase: growing up. The pattern of feeling different first emerges. Neither particularly clever, struggling with mild dyslexia, and not particularly sporty, never seeming to fit into the mainstream of family or school. Compensating by finding my own circle of friends (fellow misfits?) and by making a clown of myself to win favour by another route. Now my rebellion against my father seems but an attack on the authority, normality and the mainstream, all of which had in their turn apparently rejected me.

The second phase: off to school. Oddly, I coped with being a teenager by conforming. Peer pressure seemed now absent, expectations largely relaxed, there was freedom to explore and individuality was encouraged. Here I flourished within structures rather than against them. That feeling of difference, separateness continued, though. Even my continuing faith made me at times uncomfortable with others or others uncomfortable with me. But maybe God continued to nurture me in and through all this, while never really showing his hand.

The third phase: university. The failure to get into Cambridge was the final parental disappointment, a final break with family hopes and tradition – but my freedom oddly ensured. Freedom to be what I might want to be; freedom to work or not to work in whatever way, freedom to explore.

The fourth phase: adulthood. I had thought 'you are different' meant 'you are not so good.' It took time to disconnect those two beliefs. 'You are different' came then to mean 'you are not always the same' and sometimes even 'you are special.' And then God began to show his hand more and more: I came increasingly to commit myself to the growing sense of call and vocation. And while that marriage contract is drawn up, so many unresolved issues (authority, sexuality, autonomy among them) get left to one side or get pushed underground. Yet praise still breaks forth and I am invited to write my own Magnificat.....

Prayer

Why then does my soul magnify the Lord?
for family
for friends

for the love that I receive
for my skills and gifts
for my health and body
for my mind and its delights
for my soul and the gift of loving
for the beauty of life
for the comedy of humanity
for the glory of God
for love and light
for light and life
for love
for love

Planning & Possibilities

As well as the possibilities of meditation and contemplation for the week ahead what about writing your own Magnificat? Why might your soul presently magnify the Lord? Maybe you want to reach for your pen now or this could be a phrase to carry through the week and allow yourself at the week's end finally to let the canticle song come forth.

A review of your life could also be usefully undertaken. I happened to divide mine up in sections but that isn't necessarily the best way. You could see yours as a path from birth to the present, noting or sketching the terrain through which it has passed, a sort of pilgrim's progress. Rough, smooth, wooded, watered, arid, open, whatever. Make some notes for yourself....

Scripture

Suggested for meditation:

Psalm 139.1-18 & 23f, Ezekiel 37.1-14, Ephesians 1.3-14
Suggested for contemplation:

1. Mt 20.1-15 (abbreviated) The Labourers in the Vineyard

A landowner went out early in the morning to hire men to work in his vineyard. He agreed to pay them a denarius for the day, but about the third hour he went out and saw others standing in the marketplace doing nothing so he told them, 'You also go and work in my vineyard, and I will pay you whatever is right.' So they went. He went out again about the sixth hour and the ninth hour and even the eleventh hour and did the same thing.

When evening came, the owner of the vineyard said to his foreman, 'Call the workers and pay them their wages, beginning with the last ones hired and going on to the first.' The workers who were hired about the eleventh hour came and each received a denarius. So when those came who were hired first, they expected to receive more. But each one of them also received a denarius. When they received it, they began to grumble about the landowner. But he answered, 'Friends, I am not being unfair to you. Didn't you agree to work for a denarius? Take your pay and go. I want to give the man who was hired last the same as I gave you. Don't I have the right to do what I want with my own money? Or are you envious because I am generous?'

It's the market square of a busy town where people without work can go each morning and often obtain a day's hire. A local landowner with a large vineyard just nearby turns up to hire men to work in his vineyard, for it is harvest time. Every few hours he is out there, employing for the day those who stand and wait. Even an hour before the end of the day he's there employing the few who remain standing around. Were you to be one of those labourers, how might it have worked out for you? At what point would you have been employed and how long might you have worked? All day? Bearing the full heat of the sun? With aching back and stooped shoulders. Or maybe you just turned up half way through, worked hard enough, but had plenty of time for other things? Or were you one of the lucky ones, swanning in at the last minute? What is it usually like for you?

So the foreman calls everyone together at the end of the day and starts paying first those who arrived last, each the agreed denarius, so all are going to be paid and treated the same. As you realize this, what's your feeling and emotion? How do you react? Are you indignant, or grateful? Maybe at first you can't quite believe it? Do you express what you are feeling, your indignation or gratitude, or do you keep quiet? Do you keep in the background, or do you egg somebody else on to speak?

In the face of the complaints, the landowner says, 'Friend, I am not being unfair. You all agreed to work for a denarius, so take your pay and go. If I want to give the one who was hired last the same as I gave you, then do I not have the right to do what I want with my own money? Or are you envious because I am generous?' What is your response to that? What have generosity and justice to do with one another here and for you?

2. Mark 9.33-37 The Disciples on the Road

They came to Capernaum. When he was in the house, he asked them, 'What were you arguing about on the road?' But they kept quiet because on the way they had argued about who was the greatest. Sitting down, Jesus called the Twelve and said, 'If anyone wants to be first, he must be the very last, and the servant of all.' He took a little child and had him stand among them. Taking him in his arms, he said to them, 'Whoever welcomes one of these little children in my name welcomes me; and whoever welcomes me does not welcome me but the one who sent me.'

Once again, you find yourself with a group of disciples, and with Jesus. You have been walking and now you are resting indoors. It has been a hot day and you have been travelling in direct sunshine. It has been a day of arguments and dispute. Maybe you played a part in them or maybe you just witnessed them; arguments about who's the best, who's the most successful, who's the most gifted, who's best liked, who's the greatest.

As you sit now, you can feel the physical tiredness as the muscles in your legs begin to relax and perhaps you are slightly ashamed of the part you have played. What's your normal pattern when this sort of argument gets going? Do you roll up your sleeves and jump in? Do you egg others on? Are you a bystander, or do you withdraw in some sort of superior fashion, or do you just opt out? So when Jesus asks, 'What were you arguing about on the road?' what thoughts and feelings arise?

Certainly the ringleaders keep quiet and Jesus sighs, and sits down. 'If anyone wants to be first, he must be the very last and the servant of all', he says. And he beckons to a little child and has the boy stand there and, holding him with his arms around him, says, 'Whoever welcomes one of these little children in my name, welcomes me, and whoever welcomes me does not welcome me but the one who sent me.' So what are the priorities of God? Are you affected by what you see and hear, is any change to your thinking required? Is there anything to say to Jesus now?

3. Matthew 19: 16-22 The rich young man

And there was a man who came to him and asked, 'Master, what good deed must I do to possess eternal life?' Jesus said to him, 'Why do you ask me about what is good? There is one alone who is good. But if you wish to enter into life, keep the commandments.' He said, 'Which?' 'These:' Jesus replied 'You must not kill. You must not commit adultery. You must not steal. You must not bring false witness. Honour your father and mother, and: you must love your neighbour as yourself.' The young man said to him, 'I have kept all these. What more do I need to do?' Jesus said, 'If you wish to be perfect, go and sell what you own and give the money to the poor, and you will have treasure in heaven; then come, follow me.' But when the young man heard these words he went away sad, for he was a man of great wealth.

Jesus has been teaching in the region of Judea, across the Jordan. Pharisees and others have come and gone. His disciples are there, so are the crowd. You find yourself out in the open, among the people, not far from the river. The day is calm. People in the crowd are talking about all that Jesus has said and done. Some people perhaps are making plans to go home, while other fresh faces arrive in the crowd. Look about you, what mixture of age and sex and race is there? ..... What variety is there is people's appearance? Are these mainly country people, or town people? ...... Are you one of the crowd, or are you apart? .....

Now look for Jesus and draw closer to him. See him there with his disciples. And as you draw closer, notice the young man come up to him, and you catch him saying to Jesus, 'Master, what good deed must I do to possess eternal life?' You hear Jesus say back to him, 'Why do you ask me about what is good? There is one alone who is good. But if you wish to enter to life, keep the commandments.' The young man says, 'Which?' 'These:' Jesus replies, 'You must not kill. You must not commit adultery. You must not steal. You must not bring false witness. Honour your father and mother, and: you must love your neighbour as yourself.' The young man replies to Jesus, 'I have kept all these. What more do I need to do?' Jesus looks at the young man. How does he look? ...... What do you notice and observe? .... Is it a look of compassion or regret, of encouragement or pity, or perhaps of pure love? ...... Jesus then says, 'If you wish to be perfect, go and sell what you own and give the money to the poor, and you will have treasure in heaven; then come, follow me.' How does the young man's face seem as he hears these words unfold, as dejection comes over him and you see him turn to walk away. Notice his shoulders, ... how he stands ..... and how he walks ..... as he departs through the crowd. There is a lull now; is there anything you wish to ask Jesus? .... Or maybe you would rather talk to one of the disciples? .... Once again, allow the story to unfold. Let yourself be a part of the gospel account. Spend time near or with Jesus, talking or listening, asking or receiving ....

In a moment or two Jesus is going to turn to his disciples to speak with them and that will be the time for you to slip away, back into the crowd. What will you take away with you? .... How do you feel as you do so? .... And gradually moving back through the people, you find yourself standing where you began.

Some thoughts on… being human

We can be wisely anxious before the enormity and possibilities of God, and indeed the human ego can produce all sorts of fears and apparently good reasons for prudence and restraint, anything to avoid the pain of change and the challenge of growth. ('Why should we take Jesus as our model in this parish?' apparently one churchwarden asked of a former Bishop of Ely, 'just look what happened to him!'). Inevitably, then, risk and adventure play their part, but so too does the ever offered invitation to become more open, more willing, more supple under the hands of God. If God is to shape us, it is unhelpful if we continue to defend ourselves – as we will all do to some extent – with beliefs and attitudes that are not founded in truth. In other words, we need to become vulnerable, if he is to build his Kingdom within and among us.

But maybe we need first some different ways of understanding what it means to be human, what comprises the ingredients of our psyche. One helpful model I came across a while back is from an American Jesuit called George Aschenbrenner. This model suggests three levels of human existence, each with their own needs and giftedness. The first is the external, physical and behavioural dimension. The second is the realm of the psychological, comprising head and heart, or thoughts and feelings, the place of moods, wounds and the rest. The third and final realm is that of the spirit, of our core identity before God, our essential self if you like. I have always found this tripartite model helpful, as long as their interdependence is acknowledged, for all need respecting and engaging in the life of prayer and the journey of faith.

A second model suggests that we comprise five aspects of experience that interweave and overlap but which can be separately identified: the spiritual, psychological, biological, social and environmental aspects. So a time of grief or depression on the psychological level will have spiritual, biological, social and environmental repercussions just as physical sickness will impact on our environment and our social, psychological and spiritual selves. Any particular issue will need primarily to be addressed in the realm within which it arises or occurs, but then what we might call the aftershocks or ripple effects throughout the whole person need to be taken seriously and listened to.

But of course our human understanding has and is evolving. The revolution in psychological understanding of the last 150 years means on the positive side that we are now more informed, our perception of human experience has been immeasurably enriched and our insights into human wounding are far more sophisticated and nuanced. On the downside there has been a tendency to compartmentalize – both in understanding and in treatment – and to dismiss the value and potency of the complementary growth, and healing, that can be additionally wrought on the level of the spiritual.

We should add too something of the moral dimension here. If, through our own understanding or the teaching of the church, we have come to make a judgement about any aspect of ourselves, any pattern, behaviour or trait, there may be a tendency to leave this part of ourselves out when we come to any encounter with God – through shame, or fear, or uncertainty. But what we leave at the door of the retreat, outside the prayer encounter, will remain untouched and unredeemed by the process of the prayer. Then it will be waiting for us at the end of the time, rested and raring to go, helping to take us back as if the grace of encounter with God had never happened. So can we bring all these parts of ourselves in, let God meet all of who we are and have the capacity to be? I don't believe so much in a God who seeks always to change us, but I do believe in a God who seeks always to love us. And yet in the light of that love, fully experienced, we may suddenly find ourselves desiring to be different and then change is surely likely to occur......

Chapter 2

Lent 2 Confusion and darkness

Narrative

Three questions to ask before the cross:
- what have I been?
- what am I being?
- what could I be?

At one point a rather sardonic comment was made by Christ: 'I have spent much time cleaning up as a result of your sin.' The first sin arose from believing that I had a right to something. The serpent in the garden in the main spoke the truth. Adam and Eve had all they needed, but in reaching out also to that which they felt they also had a right to, they lost much of what they had – innocence, abundance, ease and above all intimacy with God. I have committed this sin so many times: believing I have the right to something and so reaching out and taking, while destroying something in the process. By desiring more I lose so much, especially something of the intimacy I have gained with God. Moreover, in reaching out I help suppress the truth and create a falling world with myself and human desire at its centre. In reaching out to take I grieve God and harm myself: 'My Lord, what have I been and done?'

A recurrence of my back trouble comes to seem a symbol of all that lies unredeemed within. It contributes to a day of frustration and dislocation, triggered initially by oversleeping and then an unfortunate encounter with a difficult neighbour. If I can feel like this over one day, how must God feel over his creation? Why does God put up with it as it is – and with me as I have been, as I am? 'I have done so because I love you.'

An arrangement of grasses in a blue glass jug catches my attention – each fulfilling their vocation in simplicity and beauty, and giving so much joy and pleasure at the same time. I understand so much now of the compromising of my vocation, my failures in the areas of simplicity and beauty, but do I truly feel them? I know it in my head, but do I experience it fully in the depths of my being? 'By the time I have finished with you, you will.'

I imagine I am preparing to go to confession for the sins of my whole life. I begin with a chart as I was taught all those years ago – sections of time down the left, and six headings along the top of God, family, friends, work, self, others. I catch myself thinking at one point that it isn't on the whole too bad a list after all, and a voice immediately thunders in my ear, 'Do I have to take you through the whole bloody list, step by step, line by line, sin by petty sin? We'd be here all day but we can damn well do it if we have to!' So I look more closely, tracing cause and effect, where I know them, recognizing the hurt and damage I have done others. I once thought I was loved because I was special; now I know if ever I was special it was because I was loved, love undeserved, unasked, but love nonetheless.

Prayer

Blessed lady, mother of Jesus, I turn to you now; grant me your aid. I know my giftedness – you know of my sins against your Son. I know of his love – you know of my selfishness and lack of generosity. Please ask the Father of your Son to grant me this: that I may become truly aware of the nature of my sin and to loathe it; that in loathing I may amend my life.

Blessed Lord, come to my aid, plead for me before the throne of Grace. Ask, I pray, that I may be granted a true knowledge of sin; and with knowledge, hatred; and with hatred, desire for change and a love for truth, both now and in every moment.

Merciful Father, Gracious Majesty, I pray to You in humility and in sorrow. Aid me, I beg, in my need. Grant me this: that I may know and hate my sin; that I may be strengthened to change my life; that I may have discernment in the things of the world. I pray you, hear and grant my prayer, that I be better able to serve you in love and faithfulness all the remaining days of my life. I need your help, help me now.

Planning & Possibilities

There are questions you might want to allow yourself to ask once you have placed yourself in the presence of Christ, but this time perhaps the Christ who hangs on the cross for you as for all. Three questions to ask one by one are:

- what have I been?
- what am I being?
- what could I be?

And then in due course, at the end of the prayer time, the end of the day or just on the last day, at the end of the week, hold a colloquy or conversation, but repeated three times with three different figures. One says things differently depending on who is listening – the topic of conversation is how you are, how the prayer has been. But as the conversation gets repeated, and refined, so it can deepen – and hit home the more. And each may have a slightly different response to make once you fall silent.

The traditional three are often Mary, mother of Jesus; then Jesus himself; then God our Father. But equally the Holy Spirit could be one auditor, or a particular saint important to you, or a guardian angel. But ideally a hierarchy of being should be observed – and God should always be allowed to have the last word!

Scripture

Suggested for meditation:

John 9.1-7, Luke 7.36-50, Lamentations 3.1-17

Suggested for contemplation:

1. Mark 14.32-37 The Garden of Gethsemane

They went to a place called Gethsemane, and Jesus said to his disciples, "Sit here while I pray." He took Peter, James and John along with him, and he began to be deeply distressed and troubled. "My soul is overwhelmed with sorrow to the point of death," he said to them. "Stay here and keep watch." Going a little farther, he fell to the ground and prayed that if possible the hour might pass from him. "Abba, Father," he said, "everything is possible for you. Take this cup from me. Yet not what I will, but what you will."

The scene is the garden of Gethsemane and it is beginning to get dark. It feels a rather lonely place and Jesus is there with his disciples, some other followers and you. When Jesus takes three of the disciples with him aside you may well follow too. You can see Jesus is troubled, struggling and distressed. How does seeing him like this make you feel – knowing that you can do nothing but watch and witness?

Jesus says, "My soul is overwhelmed with sorrow to the point of death, stay here and keep watch." He moves a short distance, leaving the three, his struggle continuing. Do you stay with the three or move a little towards him?

"Abba, Father," he says, "everything is possible for you. Take this cup from me. Yet not what I will, but what you will."

What happens next? What do you say or do? How do you feel? What is there to learn?

. . . .

Soon you will have to leave the garden; the unfolding story of Jesus and his disciples will continue without you. When you are ready move away, find your way back out of the garden towards the lights of the city .... and of the place in which you are sitting.

2. Matthew 26.50-56 The Garden of Gethsemane

Then the men stepped forward, seized Jesus and arrested him. With that, one of Jesus' companions reached for his sword, drew it out and struck the servant of the high priest, cutting off his ear. "Put your sword back in its place," Jesus said to him, "for all who draw the sword will die by the sword. Do you think I cannot call on my Father, and he will at once put at my disposal more than twelve legions of angels? But how then would the Scriptures be fulfilled that say it must happen in this way?" At that time Jesus said to the crowd, "Am I leading a rebellion, that you have come out with swords and clubs to capture me? Every day I sat in the temple courts teaching, and you did not arrest me. But this has all taken place that the writings of the prophets might be fulfilled." Then all the disciples deserted him and fled.

The scene once again is Gethsemane and the Mount of Olives. It is early evening. There are Jesus and his disciples, and the authorities who have come to arrest him and you. It is a scene of some confusion, with the flickering lights that have been brought against the darkness of the trees and the indigo of the sky. Indeed, as two guards move to take hold of Jesus someone draws his sword and strikes at one of the servants of the high priest.

Jesus immediately intervenes, "Put your sword back in its place, for all who draw the sword will die by the sword. Do you think I cannot call on my Father, and he will at once put at my disposal more than twelve legions of angels? But how then would the Scriptures be fulfilled that say it must happen in this way?"

One or two run to the servant's aid – maybe you too if you are close – as there is blood running down the side of his face and he is crying out in great pain.

Jesus turns to all who are gathered, "Am I leading a rebellion, that you have come out with swords and clubs to capture me? Every day I sat in the temple courts teaching, and you did not arrest me. But this has all taken place that the writings of the prophets might be fulfilled."

What are the reactions of those around? What mixture of bemusement, anger, aggression, indignation, fear, anxiety or whatever? What are you feeling?

Jesus' disciples take to their heels as the guards once more move into arrest Jesus. What do you do?

And as he is led away and the crowd disperses, what do you take away from this scene and encounter?

3. Matthew 8: 23-27 The calming of the storm

Then Jesus got into the boat followed by his disciples. Without warning a storm broke over the lake, so violent that the waves were breaking right over the boat. But Jesus was asleep. So they went to him and woke him say, 'Save us, Lord, we are going down!' And Jesus said to them, 'Why are you so frightened, you men of little faith?' And with that he stood up and rebuked the winds and the sea; and all was calm again. They were astounded and said, 'Whatever kind of man is this? Even the winds and the sea obey him.'

So Jesus is in a boat with his disciples on the lake. Jesus is settling down to rest and you find yourself in your imagination among the others with him .... Where do you find yourself on the boat? Over to one side? Or among the disciples? .... What sort of boat is it, does it have a mast, or oars, is it low in the water, or fairly substantial? .... Now look about you, what is the surface of the water like? A little bit choppy perhaps? Or at the moment does it seem perfectly still? The sky perhaps is a little overcast, but how far is the shore? What can you see as you look over the water? Maybe there are other boats around, maybe there are not ...... How does the land appear, hilly or flat, wooded or arid?

Quite quickly a storm breaks out, clouds darken even more, the waves become bigger. Hear the wind sound, feel the rain on your face. What is going on among the others? How are they responding or reacting? Do conversations break out or exclamations? How does their anxiety show itself? . . . . And look on Jesus' face as he sleeps on. Is it a deep, untroubled sleep, or it does it seem that thoughts or dreams are passing through his unconscious mind? So some of the disciples go to Jesus to wake him. How many go? Are you among them, or do you stay back? . . . . Waking him, they cry, 'Save us, Lord, we are going down!' The waves are breaking right over the boat. Jesus opens his eyes, looks about and says, 'Why are you so frightened, you of little faith?' And he stands up and rebukes the wind and the sea and suddenly all is calm again . . . . You hear a number saying, 'Whatever kind of man is this? Even the winds and the sea obey him.' Jesus settles back down. Where do you find yourself now, as the boat continues on its way through the every-calming sea? Maybe Jesus settles back down near to you, or maybe you find yourself among some of the disciples. Maybe there is a question to ask, exclamation to make, conversation to overhear, or simply to sit in silence, absorbing the wonder of all that has happened . . . . Let the story gently unfold as the boat begins to make its way to the shore.

As the sea calms, so the sky clears, and as the journey comes to an end, so you become aware that the sky is blue, the sun is shining. You can feel the warmth on your face, everything begins to dry out . . . . And you become aware it is time to take your leave, the time of travelling together is coming to an end. Is there anything finally to say or do, to hear or receive? . . . .

Some thoughts on... healing

When we think about healing we will encounter immediately the medical model that has been historically so dominant. That model of course has a stress on curing, and so sickness can come to be seen as a failure, or certainly as something undesirable and less than good. On the one hand it shows our human capacity to refuse to accept what seems less good or is deemed unacceptable, to envision alternatives and to change circumstances accordingly. Where it falls down though is when we encounter the things that can't be changed and then the obsession with trying to change the unchangeable distracts from the potential that lies rather in simple acceptance, a living with. Humanity will always have its limitations and there is an interplay to respect between struggle and acceptance.

The Christian will also need to ask what is distinctive that the church has to offer here. What can our experience of faith offer? What does Scripture have to teach? I would want to agree with the suggestion that all of Jesus' healings, as reported in Scripture, were done for the sake of the Kingdom of God. That is to say healing is not here an end in itself, and physical health is not the goal. Jesus seems to have exercised his healing ministry in order to remove obstacles to the awareness of God's presence and to facilitate a new response to the love of God. The miracles, then, were not somehow contrary to nature but actually a fuller revelation of the deep realities of a world loved by God into being.

We can look too to Jesus' own life and Passion, the unfolding story we receive, encounter and celebrate in church from the season of Advent to the feast of the Ascension. Suffering here has its own place and role and even death itself too provides a doorway to Resurrection and New life. Because of this the Church's ministry can't only be one of rescue or curing. For Ignatius Loyola, the sixteenth-century Spanish compiler of 'The Spiritual Exercises,' healing was more about raising one's awareness of where one was not whole, so that, with a fuller consciousness of our frailty and wounding, we can be the more fully open to God and more able to choose God freely and fully. Freedom here, then, is not in being healed but in having a changed and transformed relationship with our woundedness. Wounds indeed define us and give us identity and individuality, positively and negatively, and all too often it is our relationship with them or the events or people that caused them that need healing rather than the wounds themselves.

Finally, James Woodward has suggested three questions that might be of use at this point, if you wanted to take this further:

- What are the parts of our own lives that are in need of healing?
- What are the particular dimensions of the society or community in which we live that we are most aware need healing?
- In what ways is your own faith community already a healing community – and in what ways could it usefully grow or develop?

Chapter 3

Lent 3 The Light that shines in the dark

Narrative

An enactment of the parable of the Prodigal:

To claim my inheritance, I begin my naming my share of God's gifts: the people in my life I am grateful for, particular characteristics I am aware of, the hobbies and activities I enjoy, those possessions I am particularly attached to. The list seems to run for pages and runs from vocation through to gin and tonics, health to hot baths, gardening, swimming and walking to love of organizing, celadon ceramics to sexuality.

To squander all I have: What would I do if I let rip with the need to make myself popular, to feel loved and to be selfish? A cycle of spending and indulgence, the frittering away of friendships and possessions, a twenty first-century rake's progress! So easily this might have been done, I think to myself, but am brought up short by the response, "but it has happened, can't you see? Not in the same way as you imagined, of course, but each and every one of the gifts you listed have been wasted, misdirected, sacrificed in some way or another. What do you think of that?" "I am ashamed." "And so you should be."

The return: the welcome back with the divine and human as so often intertwined, the Father leading me back into the house, with his arm across my shoulders. The lamps are lit, the curtains drawn against the dark, the fire in the sitting room blazes. The house is full of all the people I rejected or used, smiling, laughing, pressing forward with no questions nor doubts but acceptance. The dogs come tumbling down the stairs in their excitement, Mary gives a yodel of celebration, a large whisky is poured and my heart is very full.

Later in the quiet I wonder about the inability fully to accept the words of forgiveness and acceptance. "If you do not believe that your sins are forgiven ask yourself why you did whatever you did, not what you did. Then you will find the way through to forgiveness and love." Mulling this over I realize sin is something much deeper than I had thought. It isn't ultimately in fact about what I have done, or not done, nor even how I have treated and used other people, serious though these all are. I always thought that in spite of these my essential self would be unaffected, unblemished. But now I realise my sin lies at the very heart of who I am and has affected, damaged my being at the profoundest level.

Sin for me, then, has been taking things for granted, God's gifts and above all his love. At heart I had made myself king of my kingdom rather than remain one of God's prophets in his world. By trying to usurp God I lost the right to be called one of the children of God. But the vision that God offers was there before and can be again – to live utterly dependent upon God and so inspire others to look to Him rather than draw their gaze to myself.

Holiness is wholeness, where to be whole is to know and accept that one is damaged, and where to be damaged is to think that one is whole. Perhaps to be holy is to accept at the very deepest level one's brokenness, for then one can truly know one's dependence on God. Here then surely is the light that can shine whatever the darkness – and where love is free to flourish, so sin can be forced to wither.

Prayer:

In this is change:
A foolish boy given wisdom?

Pride o'erthrown or selfishness toppled?
Insecurities healed or sinfulness banished?

No.

In this is change:
A beast made man and more than a man,
For like the Son of Man I am become a son of God;
And as a child of God I see all things differently,
From my place in the heart of the Creator and Lover of all.

(To be created then is to be loved,
And I am to love all created things in Him.)

For I carry God in me, and am not man nor beast,
And so in God is my being and so in this is my change.

Planning & Possibilities:

As well as the possibilities of meditation and contemplation, how would it be to enact your own 'Prodigal' story? You could use one of the coming days for it, or spread it out over the prayer times of the whole week, passing on the meditations and contemplations for a change.

- To claim your inheritance: What does it comprise? What is its extent? What can be named?
- To squander all you have: How do you and how might you do this?
- The return and the welcome back: How is it to return with nothing? How are you received?

Scripture:

Suggested for meditation:

Psalm 136. 1-16 & 23-26, Ezekiel 16.1-19, Luke 16.19-31

Suggested for contemplation:

1. John 5.2-9 The Pool of Bethesda

Now there is in Jerusalem near the Sheep Gate a pool, which in Aramaic is called Bethesda and which is surrounded by five covered colonnades. Here a great number of disabled people used to lie – the blind, the lame, the paralyzed. One who was there had been an invalid for thirty-eight years. When Jesus saw him lying there and learned that he had been in this condition for a long time, he asked him, "Do you want to get well?" "Sir," the invalid replied, "I have no-one to help me into the pool when the water is stirred. While I am trying to get in, someone else goes down ahead of me." Then Jesus said to him, "Get up! Pick up your mat and walk." At once the man was cured; he picked up his mat and walked.

You find yourself in the city by a pool known as Bethesda on the edge of Jerusalem. The pool is in the open air with brilliant white marble steps leading down to it from a covered colonnade. It's a very hot day and the sunlight reflects off the white marble and you find yourself standing there blinking against the light as you look around seeing the water lying still in the heat of the day. And as you move towards the shaded area, you suddenly become aware there is a large crowd of people lying or sitting there, in the cool. Some are on their own, some are tended by friends or relatives, some seem eager and hopeful, and others despondent. Some seem in pain, others resigned, some are asleep and others are watching.

You are aware that from time to time the surface of the water is disturbed and it is believed that those who can bathe in it at that time will be cured. How does the presence of this suffering humanity touch you? Is there anyone that you feel drawn to as you move into the shade yourself? Or maybe there is someone that you have deliberately avoided? You begin to move around the circular colonnade. Is there anyone you make eye contact with, or speak to? Or do you avert your eyes?

And you become aware that Jesus is present, moving also through the crowd, and you see him stop, stop by a man. Is it someone you have noticed before? Perhaps you even know him, or is it someone you don't recognize? Someone mentions to Jesus that he has been an invalid for many years, and Jesus asks him, 'Do you want to get well?' You hear the man reply, 'Sir, I have no-one to help me into the pool when the water is stirred. When I am trying to get in, someone else goes down ahead of me.' How does Jesus look? 'Get up,' he says, 'Pick up your mat and walk.' At this the man is transformed. What change comes over his face and expression, his body and his movements? You become aware that he was cured immediately, he is cured, for he picks up his mat and walks. What happens next? What does Jesus do? What does the man do? And what do you do?

2. Matthew 15.21-28 The Canaanite Woman

Leaving that place, Jesus withdrew to the region of Tyre and Sidon. A Canaanite woman from that vicinity came to him, crying out, "Lord, Son of David, have mercy on me! My daughter is suffering terribly from demon-possession." Jesus did not answer a word. So his disciples came to him and urged him, "Send her away, for she keeps crying out after us." He answered, "I was sent only to the lost sheep of Israel." The woman came and knelt before him. "Lord, help me!" she said. He replied, "It is not right to take the children's bread and toss it to their dogs." "Yes, Lord," she said, "but even the dogs eat the crumbs that fall from their masters' table." Then Jesus answered, "Woman, you have great faith! Your request is granted." And her daughter was healed from that very hour.

The scene is a hilltop with views over the surrounding countryside and towards a great expanse of water, possibly an inland lake, possibly the sea; a blue sky with high clouds, perhaps also a breeze.

It is a natural resting place for those walking through, and several different groups find themselves there at the same time. Maybe you are part of a group, maybe even a group that you are familiar with, or maybe you are on your own. Either way, you find yourself near Jesus and some of his followers who have just met a local woman who recognizes him.

"Lord, Son of David, have mercy on me! My daughter is suffering terribly from demon-possession." Jesus remains silent but how does he seem – does he look at her or does he look away? His disciples seem embarrassed and one or two of them say to Jesus, "Send her away, for she keeps crying out after us."

Jesus finally replies, "I was sent only to the lost sheep of Israel." But the woman draws closer and kneels before him. "Lord, help me!" she says. Jesus replies, "It is not right to take the children's bread and toss it to their dogs." "Yes, Lord," she says, "but even the dogs eat the crumbs that fall from their masters' table."

How does Jesus seem with her reply, what expression is on his face? How long does it take him to reflect and to change his mind? For he then replies, "Woman, you have great faith! Your request is granted."

The woman gets up in joy, believing and knowing that her daughter was now healed. Does she head straight for home or does she do or say anything before she leaves? Do the disciples make any comment about Jesus' change of mind. What of you and anyone you may be with – what do you observe or comment on?

The different groups begin to disperse. Jesus and his disciples prepare to continue on their way. There is one final chance now for you to go up to Jesus and say or ask anything you want. Do you take it? Or leave it for another time?

And what have you learnt here?

3. John 1.35-39 Jesus and the first disciples
On the following day as John stood there again with two of his disciples, Jesus passed, and John stared hard at him and said, 'Look, there is

the lamb of God.' Hearing this, the two disciples followed Jesus. Jesus turned round, saw them following and said, 'What do you want?' They answered, 'Rabbi,' – which means Teacher – 'where do you live?' 'Come and see,' he replied; so they went and saw where he lived, and stayed with him the rest of that day. It was about the tenth hour.

So you find yourself standing in a market square; it is mid- to late afternoon. Some stalls perhaps are beginning to open up for the evening, others perhaps remain closed. There are not that many people around. Those that are, notice what they are wearing and what they are about, whether moving purposefully, or aimlessly; maybe there are cats or dogs scavenging ...... Notice the weather, how warm it is, or overcast, and as you stand there looking about you know also that one of the people you are with is John the Baptist. He does not have your full attention and he stands there in silence.

And then you become aware of somebody striking passing by. What does he look like? How tall is he? What is he wearing? How does he move? .... And do you see John staring hard at him as he passes, and do you hear him say, 'Look there is the lamb of God'? And hearing this, a couple of you move off, following the striking man, following Jesus. Jesus turns off the market square into a narrower street, close to the dwellings and shops about you. How many storeys are the buildings? ..... In the quietness of the street Jesus is aware of you following, and he turns around. 'What do you want?' he says to you and your companion. 'Rabbi,' you find yourself answering, 'Where do you live?' 'Come and see,' he replies. What is his tone of voice? .... How confidently or softly does he speak? .... What is his expression as he looks at you? ..... He turns again and you find yourself walking with him. Do you walk behind him or beside him? .... In silence? Or maybe Jesus points out a few things as you go along. So you come to where Jesus lives. What is it like? ..... How large or small is it? .... Does he live there on his own, or does he share with others? ......

And so you spend time with Jesus in his house until evening comes. Perhaps he prepares a simple repast. Perhaps you talk. How is to be around Jesus, to spend time with him? ...... Are there things that you would like to ask, ... and how does he respond? ......

The darkness comes early to this part of the world at this time of the year, and when it comes it is time to leave. How do you take your farewell? What does Jesus say to you as you go? .... How do you feel as you walk away with your companion, back through the streets towards the market place? ...... What do you carry away from this encounter? ....

Some thoughts on... contemporary living

I have lived in cities for half my life. At the moment I live in a town – half way perhaps between the urban experience and that of the country, as well as being something in its own right. What is common to all these environments is the presence of church buildings – all shapes and sizes, ages and degrees of interest. Rarely is their location and indeed design ideal for contemporary patterns of worship or church attendance but perhaps that very inefficiency has some purpose. What might all these buildings have to say to us today, apart from being a reminder of the Church's religious and architectural heritage? Where churches are open, the interior spaces are often much used as oases of peace for numerous visitors each day. The architecture is often an invaluable part of the landscape and so perhaps a source of refreshment to the eyes as well as a reminder of the numinous for any passer-by, conscious of it or not, Christian or not. So we could start with an idea of a spirituality of place, the word made stone.

But people are the other half of the equation. The church reaches out but many people's lives remain apparently untouched. Yet many who would not necessarily be regular attenders turn to the church at particular seasons such as Christmas or times of particular joy or sorrow, and expect and find solace in the traditional forms of the Lord's prayer, familiar hymns or carols and ritual. While some may dismiss this as retrogressive, or only for those who do not take their faith journey seriously enough, it does speak, I think, of a spirituality that values elements of security, of changelessness above other aspects. All of us need this sort of thing at times but it is particularly important perhaps for those whose lives are so otherwise occupied, who confront challenge and threat on a daily basis in other areas of life. So we could think also of a spirituality of comfort, the word made rock.

But there is of course more to the landscape of the soul than that. While busyness and stress may dominate the attention, the heart is still (largely) free to register pain and hope, fear, anxiety, love and all the rest. The life of the spirit too (however that is experienced, understood or articulated) still continues its pull, trying to extend the individual's horizons, unsettling, disturbing, inviting them to reach out and stretch beyond. For many the recognition of this other dimension comes late, forced perhaps by redundancy or a breakdown in a relationship or a bout of sickness brought on by stress. It may be mediated by a crisis of meaning/lessness or struggle with depression. Others seem more naturally sensitive to the promptings of the spirit and manifest a desire to be of service somehow in their world as well as doing all they have to do on a daily basis. So, as anywhere, we can see here the search for integration and meaning, the exploring of self and selfishness and selflessness, a spirituality of becoming, the incarnating word.

Finally, we can perhaps observe here a mirror held up to our own spiritual journey in life. For we all stand with the lost innocence of Genesis on one side and the not yet realized vision in Revelation of the heavenly city on the other. The image that speaks, then, most clearly of our current human experience, caught between those two, is perhaps the market place. The pressures, stress, sheer consumerism of our contemporary western world combine to make the market place seem the perfect image for life today, whether we like it or not. For here all sorts and conditions of human experience are brought together in dialogue and disagreement, with issues of wealth, poverty, power and weakness, justice and injustice all apparently present and in tension. This market place is the locus of our human activity and so it must also be the realm of divine grace.

Moreover what we can see at work around us in our society we will sooner or later confront in our own lives, however humble, however apparently far removed from any particular madding crowd. Spirituality will also need to encompass our individual and corporate compromises and struggles, being therefore ultimately a spirituality of humanity, the word made flesh.

Flesh, rock, stone, incarnate – what is the Word for you?

Chapter 4

Lent 4 The person of Jesus

Narrative

Somehow when confronted finally by the person of Jesus words seem to fail.

I must have recited the creed thousands of times now, and all the scriptural stories are so familiar, in prayer and on previous retreats I can recall all sorts of encounters with him, meaningful and profound as well as joyous and even humourful. But having journeyed this far and in this way, this encounter today seems something completely new. I guess what I am now is not what I was then – and Jesus in his generosity and immediacy meets me always in the present.

But how to express this meeting, this renewed yet so different encounter? Being meets being, Spirit calls to spirit, heart seems to lurch and resettle into a new orbit. Things that seemed so important not even a day ago are suddenly revealed as massively irrelevant, while others that were just wrinkles on the surface of my consciousness appear in their true and significant light.

A line from John Donne's poem 'Hymn to God my God', in my sickness comes to mind: 'look, Lord, and find both Adams met in me.' The old Adam is never (alas!) obliterated but the new Adam seems increasingly at home. Who is Jesus becoming for me now? Who am I becoming for him?

Prayer

Soul of Christ, sanctify me
Body of Christ, save me
Blood of Christ, inebriate me
Water from the side of Christ, wash me
Passion of Christ, comfort me
O good Jesu, hear me
In thy wounds, hide me
From the wicked foe, defend me
At the hour of my death, call me
And bid me come to thee
that with thy Saints I may praise thee
World without end. Amen

Planning & Possibilities

How would it be to look for an image that speaks to you this week of Christ. Ask who is Jesus for you at this point and what might best represent him? It might be a crucifix or icon, a famous painting or an image that suddenly springs almost unbidden into your consciousness. You might come across a postcard that seems absolutely right or have to search your shelves or the internet for the picture you know is right but can't immediately lay your hands on.

And having found the image, sit with it, spend time with it. Find a home for it, light a candle near it, or use it as a bookmark so every time you open the book you face it afresh. Either way, live with it, share your life with it – and so live with Christ, share your life with him.

Scripture

Suggested for meditation:

Lamentations 2.19, 1 Corinthians 13.12f, Luke 22.14-20
Suggested for contemplation:

1. Luke 19.1-6 Zacchaeus

Jesus entered Jericho and was going through the town when a man whose name was Zacchaeus made his appearance; he was one of the senior tax collectors and a wealthy man. He was anxious to see what kind of man Jesus was, but he was too short and could not see him for the crowd; so he ran ahead and climbed a sycamore tree to catch a glimpse of Jesus who was to pass that way. When Jesus reached the spot he looked up and spoke to him: 'Zacchaeus, come down. Hurry, because I must stay at your house today.' And he hurried down and welcomed him joyfully.

The scene is a crowded street in Jericho. You find yourself among a crowd at a point where the street opens into a small square, in the middle of which is a large sycamore tree. It is a warm and sunny day. You sense a buzz and excitement and expectation. People know that Jesus is to pass and they want to be there to see him. Join in the excitement and find yourself among the crowd where what is about to happen is giving that sense of expectation. .... Many people now think of Jesus as the Messiah and expect the imminent coming of the Kingdom, others are simply curious to see something of this man they have heard so much about, who has performed miracles, taught with authority. Notice the crowd, the press, the street, the buildings .... And the little square with its tree. ...... How big is the tree? .... How spreading its branches? ..... How thick its leaf cover? ......

Somewhere near you someone nudges the person next to him and points out that someone has even climbed the tree to get a better view. ..... And perhaps he snorts when he realises it is Zacchaeus. .... An unpopular man, unpopular because he is both rich and a tax collector. Perhaps some disparaging remarks are passed .... Perhaps the man in the crowd even says, 'Well, there's Zacchaeus, there's one man who's not going to see the Kingdom of God.' And now the crowd's attention is clearly on the ripple of excitement that is coming down the street, following the person of Jesus and his disciples. See Jesus through the crowds, coming into view .... See how he looks, see his expression ...... Feel the hubbub and the excitement as he draws closer and closer ...... And now you see Jesus stop by the tree and look up. He has seen Zacchaeus ...... and now you hear him speak to him, 'Zacchaeus, come down. Hurry, because I must stay at your house today.' How do those in the crowd around you respond? ..... A snort of disapproval? ..... An exclamation of surprise? .... A sense of shock? ...... Zacchaeus scrambles down the tree. He needs a hand down the last bit. Perhaps you are there to help. .... Either way, you can see the joy in his face and realize that he is deeply moved. He moves to Jesus. How does he greet him? ...... Perhaps he kneels? .... Perhaps he bows? ...... Perhaps he opens his arms? ...... In his joy he does not just welcome Jesus, he welcomes the crowd, perhaps he welcomes you too, includes you? ...... Somehow you know that his life is transformed by this one simple greeting from Jesus. How does that make you feel? .... What is touched in you by this transformation? ..... Is there anything you feel you want to say to those in the crowd who are aggrieved or complain? ...... Maybe you find there is something you want to say to Zacchaeus ...... or to Jesus .... Is there something he wants to say to you? ...... Let yourself be in the moment and respond to whatever is in your heart and mind before they move off ....

Zacchaeus is going to stand his ground, but you find yourself deciding to go on ahead and so begin to prepare to make your way through the crowd, so that for now you will be ahead of Jesus. Take a last look and then turn and move off ...... Out of the little square, out of sight of the tree and of the crowd and of Jesus and of Zacchaeus, you find yourself first alone in the street, and then back where you began.

2. Mt 16.13-18 The Profession of Faith
When Jesus came to the region of Caesarea Philippi, he asked his disciples, 'Who do people say the Son of Man is?' They replied, 'Some

say John the Baptist; others say Elijah; and still others, Jeremiah or one of the prophets'. 'But what about you?' he asked. 'Who do you say I am?' Simon Peter answered, 'You are the Christ, the Son of the living God.' Jesus replied, 'Blessed are you, Simon son of Jonah, for this was not revealed to you by man, but by my Father in heaven. And I tell you that you are Peter, and on this rock I will build my church, and the gates of Hades will not overcome it'.

Once again, you find yourself among some of the disciples, and with Jesus present. This is a pause on a journey and maybe you find yourself on the outskirts of a town, with somewhere to sit and rest for a while. Notice your surroundings and how they seem to you. Maybe it's a town you know, maybe it's contemporary, maybe it's historic. Spend a moment or two looking around and taking stock before focusing more on the group of people you are with. How many disciples are present, and how does Jesus seem? Are you an observer on the edge, or in the thick of things?

And Jesus puts a question, 'Who do people say the Son of Man is?' Who pipes up? Do you say anything or do you just listen, 'Some say John the Baptist, others say Elijah and still others Jeremiah or one of the prophets, it's said.' Jesus looks around, perhaps he catches your eye, 'What about you, who do you say I am?' What do you find yourself saying quietly under your breath. Simon Peter answers, 'You are the Christ, the Son of the living God.' Jesus looks at him and replies, 'Blessed are you, Simon son of Jonah, for this was not revealed to you by man, but by my Father in heaven. And I tell you that you are Peter, and on this rock I will build my church, and the gates of Hades will not overcome it.'

Maybe you say something now to Jesus in reply to his question, to Peter in the light of what's just been said to him, to someone you happen to be near, about what you have just witnessed. Jesus asks, 'Who do you say I am?' What do those words touch in you? How do you respond to the question and to whom do you make the response?

3. John 10.10-15 'I am the Good Shepherd'

Jesus said, 'I have come that they may have life, and have it to the full. I am the good shepherd. The good shepherd lays down his life for the sheep. The hired hand is not the shepherd who owns the sheep. So when he sees the wolf coming, he abandons the sheep and runs away. Then the wolf attacks the flock and scatters it. The man runs away because he is a hired hand and cares nothing for the sheep. I am the good shepherd; I know my sheep and my sheep know me – just as the Father knows me and I know the Father.'

It is a time and place for Jesus to be speaking to you and to others. As you shut your eyes, what sort of place would be most conducive to such a meeting and some sort of instruction? A biblical scene? A room at home? Church? Let whatever scene comes to mind be there for you, however surprising or unexpected. And explore it gently in your mind's eye. Who else is there? Where is Jesus? How does he look and seem? Is he sitting or standing? What is he wearing? Where are you in relation to him?

Jesus begins to speak, 'I have come that they may have life, and have it to the full.' What is his tone of voice as he says this – stern or gentle? Is he addressing the group, or someone in particular, or is he addressing you? How do you feel?

Jesus continues, 'I am the good shepherd. The good shepherd lays down his life for the sheep. The hired hand is not the shepherd who owns the sheep. So when he sees the wolf coming, he abandons the sheep and runs away. Then the wolf attacks the flock and scatters it. The man runs away because he is a hired hand and cares nothing for the sheep.' Where is Jesus looking when he says all this? And what do his words mean for you? What do they mean in terms of your own commitments and understanding? To work, to faith, to relationships, to whatever is most pressing in your life right now?

Finally he concludes, 'I am the good shepherd; I know my sheep and my sheep know me – just as the Father knows me and I know the Father.' So what of knowledge? Knowledge of yourself?................ Of those for whom you are responsible?................ What of your knowledge of God?................ And God's of you?.............

The time is coming to a close now. What will you take away from this? Is there anything finally to say to Jesus or to let Jesus say to you? And when you are ready open your eyes.......

Some thoughts on... responsibility

As mentioned earlier there is a great debate over the precise meaning of the word 'spirituality'. One of the definitions that I continue to like is the description of spirituality as theology on legs or, in other words, lived theology. For this locates it at the nexus of theology and human experience, of ideas about God and of grounded reality and it seems to me that our own call to be people of faith in the world stands in a not dissimilar place. Experience both of God and of messy human reality come together as we explore the ramifications of being called to be disciples and apostles of Jesus in the world. So how we understand as well as experience God, and what our theology is, will therefore have a vital impact on notions of call and of our responsibility to respond to that call.

But, in very crude terms, Christian theology, in the West at least, can be seen as a seesaw between that which stresses the creation and that which stresses redemption. These are two vital Christian doctrines which need to be held in tension, but which in practical terms often see an overemphasis of one at the expense of the other. A theology of redemption tends to stress a perfect creation spoilt by a fallen world, saved by the cross of Christ, and the resulting Christian journey is then seen as a struggle to claim the efficacy of the cross and to rebuild the lost paradise. A theology that stresses creation tends to see things rather differently. In the terms of René Girard and James Alison, it can suggest that we live in a pre-forgiven universe and that our struggle to accept that we are loved and forgiven shapes us and our world and makes us in a sense co-creators. In the first model, creation begins the story, humanity's fall spoils it and redemption completes it. In the second model, redemption begins the story, grace empowers it and creation ends it. This gives rise to two different models of human response to God's call, two kinds of responsibility. I should say that I am not trying to sell a particular theology here, I am just trying to suggest that theology is never detached from Christian living and will always influence and shape our understanding, and so our choices and actions.

So maybe it's worth unpacking these suggested models further. Largely fuelled by a theology of redemption, the traditional view of human responsibility before God underlines the necessity of trying harder, of doing good or doing better, all as a matter of duty. Daily discipleship involves a struggle of dealing with the fallen world, within and without. But another view, arising more from a theology of creation, would see the responsibility of discipleship as rather about bringing into being, about co-creating, about realizing or releasing potential. This is not a matter of duty but part of celebrating, for here we are dealing with a forgiven world, a loved world. Both have their strengths and weaknesses but one may be the more needed at times to counterbalance the other, if that has been predominant in the past. For responsibility for us as Christians is the responsibility of responding to God's call, for God, for oneself and for others, and our discipleship always surely has to be seen in the light of this call to grow and develop into fuller Christian maturity.

Chapter 5

Lent 5 Desire and passion

Narrative

I find myself given a room for a quiet weekend that looks on to a wall. Irritation and resentment are my immediate response: Why oh why would they build a retreat house like this and why me? How did I end up with a room like this? But as the time unfolds I mull over my feelings and what I might learn (as opposed simply to envying those with the view!) I start by coming to see the wall as an image of sin, that which mars the view and narrows life. Also I can move the curtain so it hangs to the left not the right, making the outlook more attractive from within by masking it. I have the power, if I choose, to make the situation marginally better. And there are other ways to see the wall too. Where would we be without it? Buildings need walls; this one supports the flights of stairs. Maybe its not in the right nor the best place – maybe a slightly better designed building would internalize the stairs and free the views for everyone. The same would be true if the whole building were oriented east/west rather than north/south. So what of my structure and design? What of how my life is oriented? And if this is how I am, how much do I desire to change?

This seems somehow to be my annunciation – God's invitation and offer to me. And I am still not entirely sure what I find myself saying yes to. Might that have been true of the Virgin Mary when she said yes to the angel? Perhaps like marriage, where one says yes to a person rather than to a job, entering a covenant and not a contract? What I need then is compassion for myself and my frailties; patience with the church and the efforts of others; faithfulness to the call and the task; self-awareness and discipline; and courage in adversity. It seems a tall order! But the Spirit reminds me of much I have forgotten and out of which I forget to act. I need to 'act as if', to commit myself to ways of being and doing in keeping with the truth and reality of God's love and call. I know from my past both excessively strong and excessively weak will, and what is called forth here is pure will, that is to say God's will for me and the world and my opportunity to manifest it. But now it is not so much seeking and finding the will of God that I may do it, but rather coming to know better the will of God that I may live it. Vocation then is not so much about call and response but about falling, letting go and falling. And letting go, saying yes, means a change of heart and, in the end, of direction.

From the praying of the Office comes a further text from the early Church. 'So too souls that carry the Spirit become spiritual themselves and send forth grace upon others. This grace enables them to foresee the future, to understand mysteries, to grasp hidden things, to receive spiritual blessings, to have their thoughts fixed on heavenly things, and to dance with the angels. So in their joy unending, so in their perseverance in God unfailing, so do they acquire likeness to God, so – most sublime of all – do they themselves become divine' (St Basil the Great, 'On the Holy Spirit', chapter 9.23).

There is a chain of being and a chain of becoming. Arthur Couratin and Elizabeth Smyth variously and wonderfully parented me in faith and in belief – how might I in turn parent others in their faith?

Prayer

We beseech you, O Lord,
to continue to pour your grace into our hearts.
That as we have known the incarnation of your Son, Jesus Christ,

through the message of an angel,
so by his cross and passion
we may all be brought to the glory of the Resurrection.
Through the same your Son, our saviour Jesus Christ.
Amen

Planning & Possibilities

Perhaps begin the prayer of the week and the day by asking for the gift to see God more clearly, love him more dearly and follow him more nearly.

It is sometimes said that the three vital ingredients of the spiritual life are love of neighbour, detachment or interior freedom and humility. If any of these seem particularly problematic for you, or there is any aspect of life you would like to be different, maybe this is the time to reflect on it in prayer, to offer it to Jesus for healing. If it is an attachment or pattern of behaviour that seems unhealthy or distorted then we can even pray to God for its removal, even if a large part of ourselves may hope he isn't going to be listening....

What might in you be looking for greater freedom?

What sort of prayer might you articulate for inviting God in to help?

Scripture

Suggested for meditation:

Luke 1.26-38, John 14.15-21, John 14.22-27
Suggested for contemplation:

1. Luke 10.38-42 Mary and Martha

In the course of their journey, Jesus came to a village and a woman named Martha welcomed him into her house. She had a sister called Mary who sat down at the Lord's feet and listened to him speaking.

*Now Martha, who was distracted with all the serving, said, 'Lord, do
you not care that my sister is leaving me to do the serving all by myself?
Please tell her to help me.' But the Lord answered, 'Martha, Martha,' he
said 'you worry and fret about so many things, and yet few are needed,
indeed only one. It is Mary who has chosen the better part; it is not to
be taken from her.'*

You find yourself by a simple dwelling on the edge of a village.
You find yourself with Jesus and some of his disciples being invited
by the woman Martha into her house. How many of you are invited
in? .... What sort of room is it? ...... And as Jesus sits and begins to
speak, you notice others settling down to listen and Martha's sister
Mary sits at Jesus's feet. ..... Where are you in the room? ..... Are
you standing, or do you decide to sit? ..... What does Mary look like,
what is she wearing? .... What are you wearing? .... What does Jesus
begin to talk about? ....

Martha has been busy preparing and serving food. How aware have
you been of her busy in the background? ..... Perhaps she moves the
dishes in such a way to make some extra noise to draw attention to all
that she is about. Maybe she bustles in and out rather ostentatiously
.... Finally, when Jesus pauses, Martha interrupts, 'Lord, do you
not care that my sister is leaving me to do the serving all by myself?
Please tell her to help me.' How does Mary react to those words? .....
How does Jesus look on her? ..... Jesus says, 'Martha, Martha, you
worry and fret about so many things, and yet few are needed, indeed
only one. It is Mary who has chosen the better part; it is not to be
taken from her.'

Let the story now gently unfold. Let Martha sit down and rest
awhile, listening to Jesus who carried on speaking ..... or does she
go back about her business? ...... Does anyone else do anything?
.... Perhaps someone goes to help her? .... What do you decide to
do? .....

What does Jesus say now? ..... Soon some of you will be leaving.
Does Jesus come with you or does he stay on? ...... Maybe there
is an exchange of words at the door, maybe there is a gesture or

acknowledgement of your presence, by Mary, by Martha or by Jesus? .. .. Anyway, finally you find yourself standing once again beside the house. You go into the village. Take a moment to notice how you are ...... and then bring this to a close.

2. Luke 9.1-16 The Sending of the Twelve

When Jesus had called the Twelve together, he gave them power and authority to drive out all demons and to cure diseases, and he sent them out to preach the kingdom of God and to heal the sick. He told them: 'Take nothing for the journey – no staff, no bag, no bread, no money, no extra tunic. Whatever house you enter, stay there until you leave that town. If people do not welcome you, shake the dust off your feet when you leave their town, as a testimony against them.' So they set out and went from village to village, preaching the gospel and healing people everywhere.

The scene is Jesus with his disciples, but this time he has selected the twelve who are to be particularly sent out, to be themselves apostles. As you close your eyes do you find yourself one of them, or near them or further off? How does Jesus seem as you look about? How would you describe his mood and manner?

You are all there for Jesus to give power and authority. How does he begin? Perhaps he stretches out his arms – perhaps he raises his hand?

He speaks first to the Twelve: 'Take nothing for the journey – no staff, no bag, no bread, no money, no extra tunic. Whatever house you enter, stay there until you leave that town. If people do not welcome you, shake the dust off your feet when you leave their town, as a testimony against them.'

Now perhaps he turns to you. Perhaps he beckons you? Do you draw closer? How does he look at you? Does he reach out his hands or make some other gesture? What does he say to you? What does he suggest or entrust to you?

As Jesus turns away, what are you left with, what has Jesus given you, what risks have been taken or suggested? Spend a few moments in quiet by yourself.......before bringing this reflection to a close.

3. Luke 18.9-14 Those Praying in the Temple

To some who were confident of their own righteousness and looked down on everybody else, Jesus told this parable: 'Two men went up to the temple to pray, one a Pharisee and the other a tax collector. The Pharisee stood up and prayed about himself: "God, I thank you that I am not like other men – robbers, evildoers, adulterers – or even like this tax collector. I fast twice a week and give a tenth of all I get." But the tax collector stood at a distance. He would not even look up to heaven, but beat his breast and said, "God, have mercy on me, a sinner." I tell you that this man, rather than the other, went home justified before God. For everyone who exalts himself will be humbled, and he who humbles himself will be exalted.'

The time and place you find yourself in have been chosen by Jesus to teach and to remind. As you close your eyes you find yourself sitting down, but on what? Where do you find yourself? and with whom? Disciples, colleagues, family members – accept whoever you find there with you – and look about, explore visually your surroundings.

Jesus starts to speak – to whom does he seem particularly to be addressing his words? 'Two men went up to the temple to pray, one a Pharisee and the other a tax collector. The Pharisee stood up and prayed about himself: "God, I thank you that I am not like other men – robbers, evildoers, adulterers – or even like this tax collector. I fast twice a week and give a tenth of all I get." But the tax collector stood at a distance. He would not even look up to heaven, but beat his breast and said, "God, have mercy on me, a sinner." I tell you that this man, rather than the other, went home justified before God. For everyone who exalts himself will be humbled, and he who humbles himself will be exalted.'

What thoughts arise in you in response to what Jesus says? And what happens next in the scene? Perhaps someone asks a question and you simply witness the conversation? Perhaps you begin to talk to a neighbour? Or perhaps you and Jesus strike up a conversation?

Let the scene unfold in whatever way seems appropriate. And if there's anything you want to ask or say then make sure you ask and say it.

....

This time is coming to an end now. How will you take your leave? Is there anything finally to say or share? Will you leave Jesus and the others or will they leave you?

And open your eyes when you are ready.

Some thoughts on... sexuality and spirituality

Sexuality was associated by the early church with the fallen world. At that point the material world was seen as coming to an end, and since sexuality was largely linked with procreation and the family, there seemed little point in valuing it. In addition Jesus' own assumed singleness was taken as the preferred sign of the coming Kingdom, and we can see in Paul's letters his comments on the new form of relationships that were appropriate to the end times. All this was reinforced by the contemporary Stoic Roman belief that the virtuous state was achieved by the overcoming of the passions and pleasure. And since detachment and the avoidance of softness was seen to be the key, so masculinity became the measure of what it means to be human, and not only masculinity but virtuous masculinity too. Thus virginity becomes the ideal for both secular and sacred reasons.

We can then see in the early Christian centuries a subsequent and gradual separation of *eros* (love that is seen as passionate and particular) and *agape* (love seen as that which is universal and disinterested) in contrast to the Jewish tradition which continued to entwine the two with only one word for love. Then for the Church in the west the erotic becomes narrowly associated with the genital, and spirituality on the other hand (arising from *agape*) tends to become something that is detached and disembodied. The background perception was that both the body and intimacy were subject to decay and so are unreliable, whereas what is sacred has come to be assumed to be eternal and imperishable – and so in an odd way perhaps to be kept at a distance to preserve its purity.

Now we can see something today of the havoc this separation and alienation have wrought for society in its increasing sexualization, and isolation from the more selfless attitudes of life; for the church in her fear of sexuality and an increasing loss of generosity and humility. For we can see that sex without the sacred produces lives without connection – and ultimately a crisis of meaning and purpose; while the sacred without sex becomes ungrounded in messy reality and produces an intellectual God to whom we can only offer obedience, and so a religion reduced to moral values and dutiful ritual – and ultimately a crisis of duality.

But surely the fact of the Incarnation of Jesus, properly understood, challenges and subverts all this? There's little enough we can do for the church or the world except ask what could be done in our own life as a result. How might we allow the reunion in life and in faith of *eros* with *agape*? For perhaps our common call is to release transforming passion back into our faith, as well as selflessness back into our relationships. For sexuality, like every other aspect of human life, needs to be related to the centre and goal of life, the reign of God. If left at the door of the retreat experience or direction room it will remain unconverted.

In 1964 a church report entitled 'Towards a Quaker View of Sex' commented that 'we need a release of love, warmth and generosity into the world, in the everyday contacts of life, a positive force that will weaken our fear of one another and our tendencies toward aggression and power-seeking. We need to recognize fearlessly and thankfully the sexual origin of this force.' As we explore the role of the Trinity and the person of Jesus, the erotic force for connection and creativity empowering the divine love is hard to resist, and at its heart surely lies the journey of intimacy. John Futrell, another American Jesuit, talked of God being so carried away with love for the world that the Incarnation becomes inevitable. How might love, true and passionate, carry us away in the service of God? For once sexual passion and chastity are reunited, once *eros* and *agape* rejoined in a focused and appropriate experience of human and divine desire, who knows what might creatively and wonderfully happen.

Chapter 6

Palm Sunday Offering

Narrative

I need my ego – it brings, or can bring, efficiency, push, drive, motivation, skills, force of personality. But I need the opposite too at times – I need at times to be broken, vulnerable, dependent, hesitant, even ineffective. The ego is not my core reality and I need the ability and freedom to be all this at all times – neither one rather than the other, nor swinging from one to the other.

Perhaps sex is like the ego? The question is not whether or not it is and should be there, but rather how it is used, when and with whom, and in what way. It can be like a motor, an engine running on out of control, or an instrument, one of many means to an end, the question being how appropriately and skilfully it is directed.

Acts I.12 – 26 is the focus of my prayer at this time: the death of Judas and his replacement by election as an apostle. The election took place similarly in the context of prayer, a time of retreat. So what is dying in me, or needs to be replaced? And the disciples had to choose between Justus and Matthias in their election. What choices face me out of this dying and choosing?

As I reflect on myself I realize that what needs to be let go of now is the driven part of me that prefers efficiency over efficaciousness, goals over people, outcome over process, together with its opposite – the compulsed part of me that endures pain for pain's sake and revels in a sense of unworthiness. Both comprise two ends of the spectrum of my personality but both have also balanced and complemented each other, neither to my good. I am apparently a 'Three' on the Enneagram and it all relates to that too – indeed, I always thought Judas a good example of the same personality type. This is what should be laid to rest in Akeldama, the Field of Blood in Acts.

And what are my choices to replace all this? I take Justus as a model for justice and so the discernment that lies at the heart of true judgment: that which is right and fair. And I take Matthias as a model for mercy, the mercy that is flexible enough to cope with – indeed embrace – the change, ambiguity and mystery of life and the future: that which is generous and supple. Two good choices, but a choice must be made for fiat to become fact, for my acceptance of God's will, my offering, to become my truth.

Mulling over themes of judgement and mercy and what they actually mean or might look like, the image of pruning comes to mind. I am not particularly good on knowing or naming plants but there's a rose here that has caught my attention. A dog rose perhaps, or some old English varietal. It has a long season, blooms budding, flowering and fading at the same time. Not special, nor particularly spectacular. I have been pruned, pruned hard perhaps, and now is the time of my flowering. It will be a long season, as buds develop, open, flower and fall. I will need to watch the areas that are ready to fall and those others ready to come into bud. Not getting too attached to one part of the bush or another. Pruning may well still happen – to encourage growth, cut out dead wood or simply to improve the shape and make the whole more attractive or appropriate.

Prayer

Heavenly Father, give me grace to fulfil my calling.......
Lord, as thou wilt and as thou knowest best, have mercy.

Blessed Jesus, help me to follow your way of incarnate love.......
Lord, as thou wilt and as thou knowest best, have mercy.

In the power of the Spirit, may joyful obedience in your service be mine for ever.
Lord, as thou wilt and as thou knowest best, have mercy.

(After Andrew Clitherow)

Planning & Possibilities

Given the week ahead there are a variety of ways forward. As well as the Scripture I offer below you might want to stick more closely to the events of the week. If so a range of options occurs to me for ways of praying the Passion:

- One could chose one of the Gospel narratives, say Mark or John, and follow it through day by day.
- One could choose one of the people in the drama – Peter, Mary, whoever – and follow what happens through their eyes and experience.
- Or take whatever Jesus says and meditate on his words alone.
- Or use the liturgy of the Church as the main means of participation.

What seems right?

Scripture

Suggested for meditation:

Acts 1.12-26, John 16.5-15, John 15.1-11,
Suggested for contemplation:

1. John 4.5-15 The woman at the well

On the way Jesus came to the Samaritan town called Sychar, near the land that Jacob gave to his son Joseph. Jacob's well is there and Jesus, tired by the journey, sat straight down by the well. It was about the sixth hour. When a Samaritan woman came to draw water, Jesus said to her, 'Give me a drink.' His disciples had gone into the town to buy food. The Samaritan woman said to him, 'What? You are a Jew and you ask me, a Samaritan, for a drink?' – Jews, in fact, do not associate with Samaritans. Jesus replied:

'If you only knew what God is offering
and who it is that is saying to you:
Give me a drink,
you would have been the one to ask,
and he would have given you living water'.

'You have no bucket, sir,' she answered 'and the well is deep: how could you get this living water? Are you a greater man than our father Jacob who gave us this well and drank from it himself with his sons and his cattle?' Jesus replied:

'Whoever drinks this water
will get thirsty again;
but anyone who drinks the water that I shall give
will never be thirsty again:
the water that I shall give
will turn into a spring of living water, welling up for eternal life.'

'Sir,' said the woman 'give me that water and I shall never again be thirsty nor have to come all this way to draw water.'

So the scene is a well on the edge of a small town where villagers come to wash, fill water jars to take back to their houses, where travellers stop to be refreshed. The Samaritan woman is there, a woman who comes every day to draw water to take back to her house. .... Perhaps there is a small group of women washing their clothes. ...... It is a place of gossip and the exchange of news. And Jesus is there, too, on his own. .... You find yourself part of the picture. It is about midday. ....

And as you become aware of yourself and all around you, seeing the edge of the town a little way off and noticing what the countryside is like in this region, perhaps hearing some birdsong, feeling the warmth, the heat of the sun on your face and body, Jesus is sitting by the well. .... Notice what he is wearing, how he looks as he sits there .... Dusty and tired, perhaps, from his travels. .... The woman comes up with her water jars and you hear Jesus say to her, 'Give me a drink.' The woman is startled, she had not expected to be addressed. 'What, you a Jew, and you ask me, a Samaritan, for a drink?' You draw near to hear the full exchange. Perhaps others stop, too, and turn, caught by the unusual situation. .... Jesus says to her, 'If you only knew what God is offering and who it is who is saying this to you, you would have been the one to ask and he would have given you living water.' 'You have no bucket,' she replies 'and the well is deep. How could you get this living water? Are you a greater man than our father Jacob who gave us this well and drank from it himself, with his sons and his cattle?' What is the expression on Jesus' face as he looks back at her? .... And as he speaks, perhaps he looks around and speaks, not just to the woman but to the others there, and to you. 'Whoever drinks this water will get thirsty again, but anyone who drinks the water that I shall give will never be thirsty again. The water that I shall give will be an inner spring, welling up for eternal life.' What is your response to these words? ...... How do you feel as you hear them addressed to you? .... What does it touch in you? ..... The woman replies, 'Sir, give me that water and I shall never be thirsty again, nor have to come all this way to draw water.' She takes it on the purely practical level, the trouble it is going to save her. How do you receive what Jesus says? ...... And how might you respond when your turn comes? .... The woman for a moment busies herself with her pots and with the bucket at the well. Now is your chance to say something back to Jesus if you want, now is your chance to express what you feel, and to hear him reply to you. ......

Jesus in a minute will be turning back to the woman, who has now finished drawing water. He smiles as this encounter comes to an end. But anyway you find yourself stepping back as Jesus turns to the woman and says, 'Go home, call your husband and come back.' She replies to him, but already you are moving out of earshot. What it is that you carry away from this encounter? ..... What insight into the living water that is God's gift to you? ....

2. Matthew 11.16-19 This Generation

Jesus said *'To what can I compare this generation? They are like children sitting in the marketplaces and calling out to others:*
"We played the flute for you,
and you did not dance;
we sang a dirge
and you did not mourn". For John came neither eating nor drinking, and they say, "He has a demon." The Son of Man came eating and drinking, and they say, "Here is a glutton and a drunkard, a friend of tax collectors and 'sinners.'" But wisdom is proved right by her actions.'

The scene once again is a group of disciples surrounding the person of Jesus. Where do you find yourself this time, indoors or outdoors? An urban scene or rural? And as you begin to realize the scene, notice the mood that is around. Is it settled, or slightly fragmented? Are people calm, or a little bit nervous? Where are you in the group – a part of it, or a little to one side? Jesus is criticizing the culture of the time. 'How shall compare this generation? It's a generation that is dissatisfied and complains, finds fault, judges and misreads.

'They are like children sitting in the market places and calling out to others, "We played the flute for you and you did not dance; we sang a dirge and you did not mourn." John came neither eating nor drinking and they say, "He has a demon." The Son of Man came eating and drinking and they say, "Here is a glutton and a drunkard." But wisdom is proved right by her actions.'

Were Jesus to turn and address you, what might he say? What might he judge, what advice might he give? Let him speak to you, and if it's appropriate let a conversation unfold.....

3. Jn 21.15-17 The Questions to Peter

When they had finished eating, Jesus said to Simon Peter, 'Simon son of John, do you love me more than these?'

'Yes, Lord,' he said, 'you know that I love you.'

Jesus said, 'Feed my lambs.' Again Jesus said, 'Simon son of John, do you love me?' He answered, 'Yes, Lord, you know that I love you.'

Jesus said, 'Take care of my sheep.' The third time he said to him, 'Simon son of John, do you love me?' Peter was hurt because Jesus asked him the third time, 'Do you love me?' He said, 'Lord, you know all things; you know that I love you.' Jesus said to him, 'Feed my sheep.'

The scene is the shore of a lake, it's early morning and the sun has only recently risen. You find yourself among a small group on the shore. Some of the disciples have been fishing – perhaps you were with them? – and the net with their catch lies to one side. There is a simple charcoal fire and some fish has recently been cooked on it. Perhaps you find yourself holding a piece of bread, for breakfast has just been shared, and Jesus of course is there too. What's he wearing? How far from you is he?

And he turns to one of the disciples, Simon Peter, and says, 'Simon son of John, do you love me more than these others do?' And you hear Simon Peter answer immediately, 'Yes, Lord, you know I love you.' Jesus looks at him and says, 'Feed my lambs.' But after a pause he says to him again, 'Simon son of John, do you love me?' And Peter replies again, 'Yes, Lord, you know I love you.' Jesus says to him, 'Look after my sheep.' Then after another pause he asks him a third time, 'Simon son of John, do you love me?' Peter looks hurt and says, 'Lord you know everything, you know I love you' and Jesus turns to him and says, 'Feed my sheep.'

Could it be that Jesus will now turn to you and ask you the same question, 'Tell me, do you love me?' Were he to do so, how might you reply? And what might he then say back to you? Or notice if you feel uncomfortable – perhaps you move yourself a little further away so that an exchange with Jesus can't happen and, were you to do that, what thoughts and feelings would be there for you? What is it you might want ideally to be asked or to say? Let the story unfold in whatever way seems right.

And then become aware of the sound of the water on the shore, the breeze in the trees, the sound of the birds, as any conversation begins to come to a close.

Some thoughts on... vocation and response

The general move in the church and indeed in the world over the last fifty years or more to consider human beings as stewards of creation was, it seems to me, a vital first step in a more ecologically aware and informed spirituality. But it does often seem to remain infused by patriarchal, authoritative, all-powerful assumptions and attitudes: it still does not go the whole way in recognizing the inherent value of every life form in itself as part of God's creation. In other words, it remains *de haut en bas*. It still does not see or fully appreciate oneself or the other, all equally looked upon by the gaze of God, who says, 'This is my well beloved, in this I am well pleased.' It has taken eco-feminism to link issues of oppression and society to the wider creation and to a different approach to humanity's responsibility. Old assumptions of stewardship, involving domination over the earth and its resources, need to give way to these new insights and challenges along with the recognition that the old roots run deeper than we might think.

In the light of a more informed and theologically grounded understanding of spirituality, and in the light of a clearer understanding of our responsibility and possible ranges of response, I would want to suggest two hallmarks to look for in any vocation or call. First, that it has a mystical dimension, in other words that it values things and elements in themselves, not for what they can do; and so it fosters the awe, wonder and reverence appropriate to any aspect of God's creation and to God's presence within it. Second, that it has a prophetic dimension, that it exposes irreverent exploitation, selfishness, neglect and excess while being visionary in its call to a simplicity of purpose and the primary focus on the will of God as that which ultimately will be the most healing and most liberating of the ways available to us.

Edith Sitwell apparently once wrote, 'In the end nothing is lost, all is harvest.' I think she meant a kind of theological version of modern physics, whereby matter cannot be destroyed, but it can be either unharnessed or transformed. So we can waste, and that is one kind of harvest, or we can use and enable it to be transformed by becoming part of God's purposes. I am in the end, though, an optimist: in the end I believe God has promised nothing is lost, all will be harvest. In the light of this therefore I would want to propose that in the twenty-first century being fully human under God involves:

First, responding to the invitation to reverence and to celebrate all that we receive and experience, acknowledging that all this depends upon God for its existence and all things share their being from the same single divine source, while acknowledging the primacy of our forgiving and loving God; and secondly to acknowledge fully the implications of our own power and responsibility, by being aware of the tendency to exercise power insensitively or selfishly, and remaining open to the unique, individual and ongoing call that comes from God for our life, our prayer and this day's choices and action.

Chapter 7

Easter Day Coming home

Narrative

All that is left is the theatre of light, as the sun withdraws and the shadows rise. 'Grant me all I need' I begin my prayer. I catch myself and it becomes 'let me give all that you deserve.'

My task though now seems to be to wait quietly and to sit in the silence. Fears come and go: Might I forget again what happiness really is? Might I confuse life with gratification? Might I lose all I have been given? An old image of being a hole in the heart infant comes back to me – never feeling really loved, struggling with the insecurity that gives me. But the Father does what my father never did, or never could do. He provides a home, a place of stability, love and warmth. Not a refuge, a place of escape or rescue. But a home, from which one journeys forth and to which one returns.

So a warning plays its part. The call to shepherd means to keep watch over myself as well as over any flock entrusted to me. I need to stay conscious and alert. I name the conditions that tend to undermine me and they are boredom, pressure, anxiety, neediness, tiredness and stress. The qualities I will need to remember and work to stay in touch with to counter these are joy, watchfulness, ambiguity, mystery, freedom and simplicity. 'Be doers of the word' (James 1.22f) is my call here but for that to be held fast to requires awareness of the dangers that will threaten and awareness of the resources already given that will save.

Above all, though, is the sense of being given a home at last, a place of rest and of security. And as I carry in my heart, apparently truly for the first time, the phrase 'and the Father loves me', I realize that joy is my biggest ally, the greatest weapon the Christian and the Church as a whole has in the fight to foster, protect and proclaim all that God gifts us with – the indwelling union with Him. With joy, so many fears, anxieties and dangers are revealed in true proportion and at times as simply chimerical.

There's a passage from Gregory of Nyssa (Homily 15 on the Song of Songs) that strikes me here: 'that they may be one even as we are one, I in them and they in me...... consequently it is the person who has grown to mature manhood who has become capable of receiving the glory of the Spirit through his purity and mastery over his passions – he it is who is the perfect dove on whom the bridegroom gazes, "One alone is my dove, my perfect one." '

The journey with God over the years has brought me through so much, and through so many different ways of perceiving and experiencing Him. A father to be feared and placated, a master to be served, a hero to imitate, a son to befriend and a spirit to be unsettled by. Now how might I spell out the present? Perhaps the amalgam of lover, beloved, consoler, friend and Lord – a phrase I carry around now within and allow to echo and re-echo around.

So I ask out of the blue, 'What have I done to deserve all this?' The answer, immediately, resoundingly comes, 'Absolutely nothing!' And pushing further for an answer I come to Psalm 62 verse 11f: 'for God is powerful and very kind.' So home is finally journey's end and journey's beginning and each moment of peace and oneness encountered there is strength for a lifetime.

Rains clear, sun warms and new hope is born as shadows pass; as life is affirmed and love goes on.

Prayer

Alleluia!

Thanks be to you, O God most high, and praise be your holy name:
for all the blessings of my life
for human loving and for human friendships
for the comfort of loved possessions and comparative security
for fulfilling work and a sense of purpose
for the gift of insight and understanding
for the beauty of this world and my many interests.

Alleluia!
And let part of my praise be always offering:
compassion to others caught in the flesh
prayer out of love for all who suffer
an openness to respond to the varied needs of those around me.

Alleluia!
So let me be consumed by your love and in singleness of heart let me
follow your purposes in all things:
from maturity into old age
from health into frailty
from freedom into dependence.
Dispose all I enjoy according to your will, keep me only in this your
calling, for this vocation from you embraces all I value.

Alleluia!
Thus where you lead I may follow,
where you dwell I may live,
and that your people may always be my people
to the end of my days.
Amen – Alleluia!

Planning & Possibilities

I am sure we can recognize that love is shown primarily in deeds
rather than words, though words of love are important and have

meaning. How would it be therefore to take some time to meditate on all that God has done for you – in creation, in people, in the church, in the past as well as in the present, on this journey. And could you let yourself wallow in thanksgiving, if only for an hour? And what Alleluia might break out in response?

Scripture

Suggested for meditation:

Lamentations 3.22-28, Acts 20.26-32, John 17.11-end
Suggested for contemplation:

1. Mt 14.23-33 Walking on the Water

The boat was already a considerable distance from land, buffeted by the waves because the wind was against it. During the fourth watch of the night Jesus went out to them, walking on the lake. When the disciples saw him walking on the lake, they were terrified. 'It's a ghost,' they said, and cried out in fear. But Jesus immediately said to them: 'Take courage! It is I. Don't be afraid.' 'Lord, if it's you,' Peter replied, 'tell me to come to you on the water.' 'Come,' he said. Then Peter got down out of the boat, walked on the water and came toward Jesus. But when he saw the wind, he was afraid and, beginning to sink, cried out, 'Lord, save me!' Immediately Jesus reached out his hand and caught him. 'You of little faith,' he said, 'why did you doubt?' And when they climbed into the boat, the wind died down. Then those who were in the boat worshipped him, saying, 'Truly you are the Son of God.'

The scene is a boat on the lake. It is after dark and a group of you are crossing to the other side. Jesus isn't with you and the boat is making heavy weather because the wind is against it. You can hear the slap of water against the prow, feel the chill of the night, the lash of the wind. Maybe you find yourself helping with the rowing, or the taking in of the sail, maybe you are huddled at the back with some of the others. You are aware of a feeling of anxiety that's both within and surrounding you.

Then at some point a figure appears moving across the surface of the water. 'It is a ghost!' someone shouts. Then a cry of fear rings out. But it is Jesus and he says, 'Take courage! It is I. Do not be afraid.' Peter immediately replies, 'Lord, if it is you, tell me to come to you on the water.' And Jesus says, 'Come.' Maybe you watch Peter get out of the boat, or maybe you find yourself going yourself, walking on the water, moving towards Jesus, but then once again the fear gets the better, fear takes the ascendance. 'Lord, save me!'

But immediately Jesus reaches out his hand. 'Oh, you of little faith, why did you doubt?' And so coming back to the boat, Jesus climbs in. 'Truly you are the Son of God!' exclaim some of the disciples. Do you join in and worship? What are your thoughts and feelings as this episode comes to a close?

2. Matthew 28.16-20 The Great Commission

Then the eleven disciples went to Galilee, to the mountain where Jesus had told them to go. When they saw him, they worshipped him; but some doubted. Then Jesus came to them and said, 'All authority in heaven and on earth has been given to me. Therefore go and make disciples of all nations, baptizing them in the name of the Father and of the Son and of the Holy Spirit, and teaching them to obey everything I have commanded you. And surely I am with you always, to the very end of the age.'

The place you find yourself in is one of the high places – perhaps one familiar to you, perhaps not. It is the place and time of Jesus taking his farewell from his disciples. What is the scene actually like? What time of day? Morning, afternoon, evening? What lies around? What can you see? What is the weather like? How many people are there? How are they dressed and how do they seem?

Jesus appears, bearing the marks of the crucifixion, and many fall to their knees before him. Where are you standing in relation to him, what do you do as he appears? Jesus speaks to the eleven disciples before him, 'All authority in heaven and on earth has been given to me. Therefore go and make disciples of all nations, baptizing them in the name of the Father and of the Son and of the Holy Spirit, and teaching them to obey everything I have commanded you. And surely I am with you always, to the very end of the age.'

These disciples are now apostles, sent out by Jesus. What do you see as having happened between them here? How do the disciples seem or appear now?

.... And what of you? Has Jesus anything to say to you? To entrust you with? What, if anything, happens between you now?

.... And as the time comes for Jesus to depart what do the disciples do? And the rest of Jesus' followers present? What of those who doubted? And what of you – how do you take your leave?

3. John 3.25-32 John the Baptist
An argument developed between some of John's disciples and a certain Jew over the matter of ceremonial washing. They came to John and said to him, 'Rabbi, that man who was with you on the other side of the Jordan – the one you testified about – well, he is baptizing, and everyone is going to him.' To this John replied, 'A man can receive only what is given him from heaven. You yourselves can testify that I said, "I am not the Christ but am sent ahead of him." The bride belongs to the bridegroom. The friend who attends the bridegroom waits and listens for him, and is full of joy when he hears the bridegroom's voice. That joy is mine, and it is now complete. He must become greater; I must become less.'

John the Baptist is approached by some of his own disciples – how old are they and what does he look like? What are they wearing – how are they dressed? What sort of place do you find yourself in as you observe their meeting?

One of the disciples speaks, 'Rabbi, that man who was with you on the other side of the Jordan – the one you testified about – well, he is baptizing, and everyone is going to him.' What tone of voice does he use? Do you need to draw closer to hear more clearly? Does John notice you or is he intent upon the questioner and the others?

John replies, 'A man can receive only what is given him from heaven. You yourselves can testify that I said, "I am not the Christ but am sent ahead of him." The bride belongs to the bridegroom. The friend who attends the bridegroom waits and listens for him, and is full of joy when he hears the bridegroom's voice.' How does John seem as he says this – what is his manner and how does he come across?

What in all this particularly strikes you – what is said, or how it is said, or seeing John with his followers or whatever? John concludes, 'That joy is mine, and it is now complete. He must become greater; I must become less.' What of John's spirit is particularly communicated to you here – his joy? His focus on Jesus? His certainty? His passion? What? Is there anything you want to ask or say or do? Might John have anything to say to you? Let what needs or wants to happen, happen...........

And when you are ready be aware that this encounter must now begin to draw to a close, how might it end, what is your way back to the present and the here and now?

More thoughts on... prayer

The Examination of Conscience is an ancient tool of prayer and the spiritual life, but there has been a trend over recent decades to expand its focus from conscience to consciousness, from a greater awareness of sin to a greater awareness full stop; an awareness that will include sin but also grace, resulting in rejoicing as well as sorrow – surely appropriate for a people called to bear witness to and live out the mystery and wonder of Easter.

This shift from Examination of Conscience to Examen of Consciousness is perhaps witness to a wider shift away from an objective morality of action to an informed subjective morality of person. By this I mean that personal unfreedom and inordinate interior attachments aren't judged against a rule book but are set within the whole of an individual's relationship with the God of Jesus Christ, incarnate and risen, with the Father prodigal of love. As John Climacus comments in his 'Ladder of Divine Perfection', God waits not so much for a right conclusion about a practical matter facing us as our suppleness in falling into the divine hands so that God can work in us.

The Examen has still – in my experience – not really caught on outside certain circles. Its traditional structure can seem cumbersome and off-putting. Even as a daily discipline it may not be sufficient in fostering the supple awareness and sensitivity that is sought in ever more fully identifying the ways of the working of the Holy Spirit in our story and all that operates to hinder the possibilities of new life.

Some additionally may find its stress on introspection makes its use appear laborious or selfish. But against that I would suggest that our self or soul needs to be nurtured and shaped because we are always in the process of being formed, as humans, as disciples, as apostles. Our ability to be aware needs refining; our skill in co-ordination and integration needs fostering. In one sense, as I have suggested before, we are a co-creator. Just as one of the creation accounts in Genesis sees God as brooding over the waters, and then ordering and bringing forth, so the self or soul must order and bring forth the unconscious elements within our own personality. Thus interior entropy is reduced and energy will be used more creatively: conflictive thoughts can be harmonized; meaning can be discovered in any and all of the chance events or life; and there will be the possibility of a reconciliation between our chosen goals and the natural forces of life.

For Dietrich Bonhoeffer the strictly ethical life needs always to be relativized; even when we have courageously to grasp reality and take hard, ambiguous decisions, our life remains 'wonderfully enfolded by good powers,' to quote his final poem. Hence we can always move forward in trust and hope, for him in the chaos of Germany in 1945, for us in the chaos of life today.

There will always be believers who condemn introspection, who are therefore uneasy with the insights of psychology, and who avoid the Examen and similar prayer exercises. But faith-full introspection grounds our experience in those greater good powers and can radically transform our perspective. As Harry Williams reminds us in his book 'True Resurrection':

> ... theological enquiry is basically related to self-awareness and therefore it involves a process of self-discovery, so that, whatever else theology is, it must in some sense be a theology of the self.

Given that Christianity proclaims a God whose own self is irrevocably committed to the human, we surely cannot make too sharp a disjunction between what is human and what is divine. Our reflections on the nature of our God will always have immediate and personal implications for our lives. Conversely, our reflection on ourselves and on how we have spent our time will always be saying something about God. Thus the Examen helps us discern the good forces that are at work in the conscious and unconscious processes of our lives and how we remain individually and corporately wonderfully enfolded.

Conclusion

Now a retreat completed is never something finished. All that has been brought to the surface, positive and negative, will need to be integrated and deepened as one returns to ordinary life, home, work, relationships. This may involve adapting one's pattern of daily or weekly prayer, responding to an awareness or insight received. It may also result in a commitment to further exploration with another person or in some group. For the journey continues on, and may well need to be supported by our churches and faith communities, by our pattern of daily prayer and by the meaningful conversations that allow us to continue to reflect more clearly on the presence of God and all that might stand in the way of our more generous responding to his love.

Christian formation can and does take place without spiritual direction and without the experience of retreats, just as gardens can grow without compost and fertilizer. God continues to show remarkable patience with our short-sightedness and wilfulness, often allowing them to run their course, while remaining faithful and attentive himself. But authentic formation will never allow us to continue the habit of ostriches, burying our head in whatever social or ecclesiastical sand lies to hand. What constitutes spiritual direction or accompaniment will in large part arise not only from the background, experience and training of the director and the understanding, hopes and expectations of the directee, but also what arises from the relationship that will develop over time between the two as they meet in the presence of the Holy Spirit of God. The director in all this may take a variety of roles, ranging from father/mother to mentor, pastor, teacher; from guide and soul friend through to confessor or counsellor. But the horizon in all these will remain the following of the prompting of the Spirit in the ongoing conversion or transformation of the human soul after the pattern of Christ in the service of the Kingdom of God. Difficulties may of course arise in this process, be that difficulties in the relationship between director and directee, struggles with internal blocks and resistances, or simply arising from the encounter with the mystery of sin and evil in the world and in the human heart. Were however difficulties not to appear one would wonder about the value of the endeavour; and indeed how those difficulties are dealt with has the potential of shaping creatively or destructively the ongoing story.

For the authentic process of spiritual direction is surely like the formation we undergo within the journey of faith, formation as Christians, as human beings, as children of God: a process of becoming, becoming what we contemplate in the Church, becoming what we contemplate in the Christ made human for us.

And this is often where the practice of spiritual accompaniment and regular retreat comes in. Authentic formation, nourished by the support of others and the richness of our Christian heritage, is in the end the only possible response to the person of Jesus Christ, the Word of God who has pitched his tent among us irrevocably.

Finally, three questions:

- What aspect of your life or giftedness or abilities or experience has been brought to your attention over the last few weeks that is calling for acceptance or particular celebration at the moment?
- Are there any unhealthy or unhelpful patterns within or without that you have become aware of that you have or might have a tendency towards that could usefully now be addressed?
- As Eastertide unfolds, to what might you be being called that will build on and develop all you have done and been graced with on this Lenten journey of retreat?

APPENDIX: Scripture passages for Meditation

Ash Wednesday   Re-encountering God

Psalm 104, Philippians 3.7-14

Psalm 104
¹Praise the LORD, my soul.
 LORD my God, you are very great;
 you are clothed with splendour and majesty.
²The LORD wraps himself in light as with a garment;
 he stretches out the heavens like a tent
³and lays the beams of his upper chambers on their waters.
 He makes the clouds his chariot
 and rides on the wings of the wind.
⁴He makes winds his messengers,
 flames of fire his servants.
⁵He set the earth on its foundations;
 it can never be moved.
⁶You covered it with the watery depths as with a garment;
 the waters stood above the mountains.
⁷But at your rebuke the waters fled,
 at the sound of your thunder they took to flight;

⁸they flowed over the mountains,
  they went down into the valleys,
  to the place you assigned for them.
⁹You set a boundary they cannot cross;
  never again will they cover the earth.
¹⁰He makes springs pour water into the ravines;
  it flows between the mountains.
¹¹They give water to all the beasts of the field;
  the wild donkeys quench their thirst.
¹²The birds of the sky nest by the waters;
  they sing among the branches.
¹³He waters the mountains from his upper chambers;
  the land is satisfied by the fruit of his work.
¹⁴He makes grass grow for the cattle,
  and plants for people to cultivate,
  bringing forth food from the earth:
¹⁵wine that gladdens human hearts,
  oil to make their faces shine,
  and bread that sustains their hearts.
¹⁶The trees of the LORD are well-watered,
  the cedars of Lebanon that he planted.
¹⁷There the birds make their nests;
  the stork has its home in the junipers.
¹⁸The high mountains belong to the wild goats;
  the crags are a refuge for the hyrax.
¹⁹He made the moon to mark the seasons,
  and the sun knows when to go down.
²⁰You bring darkness, it becomes night,
  and all the beasts of the forest prowl.
²¹The lions roar for their prey
  and seek their food from God.
²²The sun rises, and they steal away;
  they return and lie down in their dens.

²³Then people go out to their work,
 to their labour until evening.
²⁴How many are your works, LORD!
 In wisdom you made them all;
 the earth is full of your creatures.
²⁵There is the sea, vast and spacious,
 teeming with creatures beyond number,
 living things both large and small.
²⁶There the ships go to and fro,
 and Leviathan, which you formed to frolic there.
²⁷All creatures look to you
 to give them their food at the proper time.
²⁸When you give it to them,
 they gather it up;
 when you open your hand,
 they are satisfied with good things.
²⁹When you hide your face,
 they are terrified;
 when you take away their breath,
 they die and return to the dust.
³⁰When you send your Spirit,
 they are created,
 and you renew the face of the ground.
³¹May the glory of the LORD endure forever;
 may the LORD rejoice in his works,
³²he who looks at the earth, and it trembles,
 who touches the mountains, and they smoke.
³³I will sing to the LORD all my life;
 I will sing praise to my God as long as I live.
³⁴May my meditation be pleasing to him,
 as I rejoice in the LORD.
³⁵But may sinners vanish from the earth
 and the wicked be no more.
 Praise the LORD, my soul.
 Praise the LORD.

Philippians 3
[7]But whatever were gains to me I now consider loss for the sake of Christ. [8] What is more, I consider everything a loss because of the surpassing worth of knowing Christ Jesus my Lord, for whose sake I have lost all things. I consider them garbage, that I may gain Christ[9] and be found in him, not having a righteousness of my own that comes from the law, but that which is through faith in Christ; the righteousness that comes from God on the basis of faith.[10] I want to know Christ – yes, to know the power of his resurrection and participation in his sufferings, becoming like him in his death,[11] and so, somehow, attaining to the resurrection from the dead.

[12]Not that I have already obtained all this, or have already arrived at my goal, but I press on to take hold of that for which Christ Jesus took hold of me.[13] Brothers and sisters, I do not consider myself yet to have taken hold of it. But one thing I do: forgetting what is behind and straining towards what is ahead,[14] I press on towards the goal to win the prize for which God has called me heavenward in Christ Jesus.

Lent 1   Discovering myself

Psalm 139.1-16 & 23f, Ezekiel 37.1-14, Ephesians 1.3-14

Psalm 139.1-16 & 23f
[1]You have searched me, LORD,
  and you know me.
[2]You know when I sit and when I rise;
  you perceive my thoughts from afar.
[3]You discern my going out and my lying down;
  you are familiar with all my ways.
[4]Before a word is on my tongue
  you, LORD, know it completely.
[5]You hem me in behind and before,
  and you lay your hand upon me.

⁶Such knowledge is too wonderful for me,
too lofty for me to attain.
⁷Where can I go from your Spirit?
Where can I flee from your presence?
⁸If I go up to the heavens, you are there;
if I make my bed in the depths, you are there.
⁹If I rise on the wings of the dawn,
if I settle on the far side of the sea,
¹⁰even there your hand will guide me,
your right hand will hold me fast.
¹¹If I say, 'Surely the darkness will hide me
and the light become night around me',
¹²even the darkness will not be dark to you;
the night will shine like the day,
for darkness is as light to you.
¹³For you created my inmost being;
you knit me together in my mother's womb.
¹⁴I praise you because I am fearfully and wonderfully made;
your works are wonderful,
I know that full well.
¹⁵My frame was not hidden from you
when I was made in the secret place,
when I was woven together in the depths of the earth.
¹⁶Your eyes saw my unformed body;
all the days ordained for me were written in your book
before one of them came to be.
²³Search me, God, and know my heart;
test me and know my anxious thoughts.
²⁴See if there is any offensive way in me,
and lead me in the way everlasting.

Ezekiel 37.1-14
¹The hand of the LORD was on me, and he brought me out by the Spirit of the LORD and set me in the middle of a valley; it was full

of bones.[2] He led me back and forth among them, and I saw a great many bones on the floor of the valley, bones that were very dry.[3] He asked me, 'Son of man, can these bones live?'

I said, 'Sovereign LORD, you alone know.'

[4]Then he said to me, 'Prophesy to these bones and say to them, "Dry bones, hear the word of the LORD![5] This is what the Sovereign LORD says to these bones: I will make breath enter you, and you will come to life.[6] I will attach tendons to you and make flesh come upon you and cover you with skin; I will put breath in you, and you will come to life. Then you will know that I am the LORD." '

[7]So I prophesied as I was commanded. And as I was prophesying, there was a noise, a rattling sound, and the bones came together, bone to bone.[8] I looked, and tendons and flesh appeared on them and skin covered them, but there was no breath in them.

[9]Then he said to me, 'Prophesy to the breath; prophesy, son of man, and say to it, "This is what the Sovereign LORD says: Come, breath, from the four winds and breathe into these slain, that they may live." '[10] So I prophesied as he commanded me, and breath entered them; they came to life and stood up on their feet: a vast army.

[11]Then he said to me: 'Son of man, these bones are the people of Israel. They say, "Our bones are dried up and our hope is gone; we are cut off."[12] Therefore prophesy and say to them: "This is what the Sovereign LORD says: My people, I am going to open your graves and bring you up from them; I will bring you back to the land of Israel.[13] Then you, my people, will know that I am the LORD, when I open your graves and bring you up from them.[14] I will put my Spirit in you and you will live, and I will settle you in your own land. Then you will know that I the LORD have spoken, and I have done it, declares the LORD." '

Ephesians 1.3-14

[3]Praise be to the God and Father of our Lord Jesus Christ, who has blessed us in the heavenly realms with every spiritual blessing in Christ.[4] For he chose us in him before the creation of the world to

be holy and blameless in his sight. In love[5] he predestined us for adoption to sonship through Jesus Christ, in accordance with his pleasure and will,[6] to the praise of his glorious grace, which he has freely given us in the One he loves.[7] In him we have redemption through his blood, the forgiveness of sins, in accordance with the riches of God's grace[8] that he lavished on us. With all wisdom and understanding,[9] he made known to us the mystery of his will according to his good pleasure, which he purposed in Christ,[10] to be put into effect when the times reach their fulfilment, to bring unity to all things in heaven and on earth under Christ.

[11]In him we were also chosen, having been predestined according to the plan of him who works out everything in conformity with the purpose of his will,[12] in order that we, who were the first to put our hope in Christ, might be for the praise of his glory.[13] And you also were included in Christ when you heard the message of truth, the gospel of your salvation. When you believed, you were marked in him with a seal, the promised Holy Spirit,[14] who is a deposit guaranteeing our inheritance until the redemption of those who are God's possession, to the praise of his glory.

Lent 2   Confusion and darkness

John 9.1-7, Luke 7.36-50, Lamentations 3.1-17

John 9.1-7

[1]As he went along, he saw a man blind from birth.[2] His disciples asked him, 'Rabbi, who sinned, this man or his parents, that he was born blind?'

[3]'Neither this man nor his parents sinned,' said Jesus, 'but this happened so that the works of God might be displayed in him.[4] As long as it is day, we must do the works of him who sent me. Night is coming, when no one can work.[5] While I am in the world, I am the light of the world.'

[6]After saying this, he spit on the ground, made some mud with the saliva, and put it on the man's eyes.[7] 'Go,' he told him, 'wash in

the Pool of Siloam' (this word means 'Sent'). So the man went and washed, and came home seeing.

Luke 7.36-50

[36]When one of the Pharisees invited Jesus to have dinner with him, he went to the Pharisee's house and reclined at the table.[37] A woman in that town who lived a sinful life learned that Jesus was eating at the Pharisee's house, so she came there with an alabaster jar of perfume.[38] As she stood behind him at his feet weeping, she began to wet his feet with her tears. Then she wiped them with her hair, kissed them and poured perfume on them.

[39]When the Pharisee who had invited him saw this, he said to himself, 'If this man were a prophet, he would know who is touching him and what kind of woman she is, that she is a sinner.'

[40]Jesus answered him, 'Simon, I have something to tell you.'

'Tell me, teacher,' he said.

[41]'Two people owed money to a certain moneylender. One owed him five hundred denarii, and the other fifty.[42] Neither of them had the money to pay him back, so he forgave the debts of both. Now which of them will love him more?'

[43]Simon replied, 'I suppose the one who had the bigger debt forgiven.'

'You have judged correctly,' Jesus said.

[44]Then he turned towards the woman and said to Simon, 'Do you see this woman? I came into your house. You did not give me any water for my feet, but she wet my feet with her tears and wiped them with her hair.[45] You did not give me a kiss, but this woman, from the time I entered, has not stopped kissing my feet.[46] You did not put oil on my head, but she has poured perfume on my feet.[47] Therefore, I tell you, her many sins have been forgiven, as her great love has shown. But whoever has been forgiven little loves little.'

[48]Then Jesus said to her, 'Your sins are forgiven.'

[49]The other guests began to say among themselves, 'Who is this who even forgives sins?'

[50]Jesus said to the woman, 'Your faith has saved you; go in peace.'

Lamentations 3.1-17

[1]I am the man who has seen affliction
by the rod of the Lord's wrath.

[2]He has driven me away and made me walk
in darkness rather than light;

[3]indeed, he has turned his hand against me
again and again, all day long.

[4]He has made my skin and my flesh grow old
and has broken my bones.

[5]He has besieged me and surrounded me
with bitterness and hardship.

[6]He has made me dwell in darkness
like those long dead.

[7]He has walled me in so I cannot escape;
he has weighed me down with chains.

[8]Even when I call out or cry for help,
he shuts out my prayer.

[9]He has barred my way with blocks of stone;
he has made my paths crooked.

[10]Like a bear lying in wait,
like a lion in hiding,

[11]he dragged me from the path and mangled me
and left me without help.

[12]He drew his bow
and made me the target for his arrows.

[13]He pierced my heart
with arrows from his quiver.

[14]I became the laughing-stock of all my people;
they mock me in song all day long.

[15]He has filled me with bitter herbs
and given me gall to drink.

[16]He has broken my teeth with gravel;
he has trampled me in the dust.

[17]I have been deprived of peace;
I have forgotten what prosperity is.

Lent 3   The Light that shines in the dark

Psalm 136.1-16 & 23-26, Ezekiel 16.1-22, Luke 16.19-31

Psalm 136.1-16 & 23-26

¹Give thanks to the LORD, for he is good.
His love endures forever.
²Give thanks to the God of gods.
His love endures forever.
³Give thanks to the Lord of lords:
His love endures forever.
⁴to him who alone does great wonders,
His love endures forever.
⁵who by his understanding made the heavens,
His love endures forever.
⁶who spread out the earth upon the waters,
His love endures forever.
⁷who made the great lights –
His love endures forever.
⁸the sun to govern the day,
His love endures forever.
⁹the moon and stars to govern the night;
His love endures forever.
¹⁰to him who struck down the firstborn of Egypt
His love endures forever.
¹¹and brought Israel out from among them
His love endures forever.
¹²with a mighty hand and outstretched arm;
His love endures forever.
¹³to him who divided the Red Sea asunder
His love endures forever.
¹⁴and brought Israel through the midst of it,
His love endures forever.

[15]but swept Pharaoh and his army into the Red Sea;
His love endures forever.
[16]to him who led his people through the wilderness;
His love endures forever.
[23]He remembered us in our low estate
His love endures forever.
[24]and freed us from our enemies.
His love endures forever.
[25]He gives food to every creature.
His love endures forever.
[26]Give thanks to the God of heaven.
His love endures forever.

Ezekiel 16.1-19

[1]The word of the LORD came to me:[2] 'Son of man, confront Jerusalem with her detestable practices[3] and say, "This is what the Sovereign LORD says to Jerusalem: Your ancestry and birth were in the land of the Canaanites; your father was an Amorite and your mother a Hittite.[4] On the day you were born your cord was not cut, nor were you washed with water to make you clean, nor were you rubbed with salt or wrapped in cloths.[5] No one looked on you with pity or had compassion enough to do any of these things for you. Rather, you were thrown out into the open field, for on the day you were born you were despised.

[6] "Then I passed by and saw you kicking about in your blood, and as you lay there in your blood I said to you, 'Live!'[7] I made you grow like a plant of the field. You grew and developed and entered puberty. Your breasts had formed and your hair had grown, yet you were stark naked.

[8] "Later I passed by, and when I looked at you and saw that you were old enough for love, I spread the corner of my garment over you and covered your naked body. I gave you my solemn oath and entered into a covenant with you, declares the Sovereign LORD, and you became mine.

[9] "I bathed you with water and washed the blood from you and put ointments on you.[10] I clothed you with an embroidered dress

and put sandals of fine leather on you. I dressed you in fine linen and covered you with costly garments.[11] I adorned you with jewellery: I put bracelets on your arms and a necklace around your neck,[12] and I put a ring on your nose, earrings on your ears and a beautiful crown on your head.[13] So you were adorned with gold and silver; your clothes were of fine linen and costly fabric and embroidered cloth. Your food was honey, olive oil and the finest flour. You became very beautiful and rose to be a queen.[14] And your fame spread among the nations on account of your beauty, because the splendour I had given you made your beauty perfect, declares the Sovereign LORD.

[15] "But you trusted in your beauty and used your fame to become a prostitute. You lavished your favours on anyone who passed by and your beauty became his.[16] You took some of your garments to make gaudy high places, where you carried on your prostitution. You went to him, and he possessed your beauty.[17] You also took the fine jewellery I gave you, the jewellery made of my gold and silver, and you made for yourself male idols and engaged in prostitution with them.[18] And you took your embroidered clothes to put on them, and you offered my oil and incense before them.[19] Also the food I provided for you – the flour, olive oil and honey I gave you to eat – you offered as fragrant incense before them." That is what happened,' declares the Sovereign LORD.

Luke 16.19-31

Jesus said,[19] 'There was a rich man who was dressed in purple and fine linen and lived in luxury every day.[20] At his gate was laid a beggar named Lazarus, covered with sores[21] and longing to eat what fell from the rich man's table. Even the dogs came and licked his sores.

[22] 'The time came when the beggar died and the angels carried him to Abraham's side. The rich man also died and was buried.[23] In Hades, where he was in torment, he looked up and saw Abraham far away, with Lazarus by his side.[24] So he called to him, "Father Abraham, have pity on me and send Lazarus to dip the tip of his finger in water and cool my tongue, because I am in agony in this fire."

²⁵'But Abraham replied, "Son, remember that in your lifetime you received your good things, while Lazarus received bad things, but now he is comforted here and you are in agony.²⁶ And besides all this, between us and you a great chasm has been set in place, so that those who want to go from here to you cannot, nor can anyone cross over from there to us."

²⁷'He answered, "Then I beg you, father, send Lazarus to my family,²⁸ for I have five brothers. Let him warn them, so that they will not also come to this place of torment."

²⁹'Abraham replied, "They have Moses and the Prophets; let them listen to them."

³⁰'"No, father Abraham," he said, "but if someone from the dead goes to them, they will repent."

³¹'He said to him, "If they do not listen to Moses and the Prophets, they will not be convinced even if someone rises from the dead."'

Lent 4   The person of Jesus

Lamentations 2.19, 1 Corinthians 13.12f, Luke 22.14-20

Lamentations 2.19

¹⁹Arise, cry out in the night,
  as the watches of the night begin;
  pour out your heart like water
  in the presence of the Lord.

1 Corinthians 13.12f

¹²For now we see only a reflection as in a mirror; then we shall see face to face. Now I know in part; then I shall know fully, even as I am fully known.

¹³And now these three remain: faith, hope and love. But the greatest of these is love.

Luke 22.14-20

[14]When the hour came, Jesus and his apostles reclined at the table.[15] And he said to them, 'I have eagerly desired to eat this Passover with you before I suffer.[16] For I tell you, I will not eat it again until it finds fulfilment in the kingdom of God.'

[17]After taking the cup, he gave thanks and said, 'Take this and divide it among you.[18] For I tell you I will not drink again from the fruit of the vine until the kingdom of God comes.'

[19]And he took bread, gave thanks and broke it, and gave it to them, saying, 'This is my body given for you; do this in remembrance of me.'

[20]In the same way, after the supper he took the cup, saying, 'This cup is the new covenant in my blood, which is poured out for you.'

Lent 5   Desire and Passion

Luke 1.26-38, John 14.15-21, John 14.21-27

Luke 1.26-38

[26]In the sixth month of Elizabeth's pregnancy, God sent the angel Gabriel to Nazareth, a town in Galilee,[27] to a virgin pledged to be married to a man named Joseph, a descendant of David. The virgin's name was Mary.[28] The angel went to her and said, 'Greetings, you who are highly favoured! The Lord is with you.'

[29]Mary was greatly troubled at his words and wondered what kind of greeting this might be.[30] But the angel said to her, 'Do not be afraid, Mary; you have found favour with God.[31] You will conceive and give birth to a son, and you are to call him Jesus.[32] He will be great and will be called the Son of the Most High. The Lord God will give him the throne of his father David,[33] and he will reign over Jacob's descendants forever; his kingdom will never end.'

[34]'How will this be,' Mary asked the angel, 'since I am a virgin?'

[35]The angel answered, 'The Holy Spirit will come on you, and the power of the Most High will overshadow you. So the holy one to be

born will be called the Son of God.[36] Even Elizabeth your relative is going to have a child in her old age, and she who was said to be unable to conceive is in her sixth month.[37] For no word from God will ever fail.'

[38]'I am the Lord's servant,' Mary answered. 'May your word to me be fulfilled.' Then the angel left her.

John 14.15-21

Jesus said,[15] 'If you love me, keep my commands.[16] And I will ask the Father, and he will give you another advocate to help you and be with you forever –[17] the Spirit of truth. The world cannot accept him, because it neither sees him nor knows him. But you know him, for he lives with you and will be in you.[18] I will not leave you as orphans; I will come to you.[19] Before long, the world will not see me any more, but you will see me. Because I live, you also will live.[20] On that day you will realize that I am in my Father, and you are in me, and I am in you.[21] Whoever has my commands and keeps them is the one who loves me. The one who loves me will be loved by my Father, and I too will love them and show myself to them.'

John 14.22-27

[22]Then Judas (not Judas Iscariot) said, 'But, Lord, why do you intend to show yourself to us and not to the world?'

[23]Jesus replied, 'Anyone who loves me will obey my teaching. My Father will love them, and we will come to them and make our home with them.[24] Anyone who does not love me will not obey my teaching. These words you hear are not my own; they belong to the Father who sent me.

[25]'All this I have spoken while still with you.[26] But the Advocate, the Holy Spirit, whom the Father will send in my name, will teach you all things and will remind you of everything I have said to you.[27] Peace I leave with you; my peace I give you. I do not give to you as the world gives. Do not let your hearts be troubled and do not be afraid.'

Palm Sunday   Offering

Acts 1.12-26, John 16.5-15, John 15.1-11

Acts 1.12-26

[12]Then the apostles returned to Jerusalem from the hill called the Mount of Olives, a Sabbath day's walk from the city.[13] When they arrived, they went upstairs to the room where they were staying. Those present were Peter, John, James and Andrew; Philip and Thomas, Bartholomew and Matthew; James son of Alphaeus and Simon the Zealot, and Judas son of James.[14] They all joined together constantly in prayer, along with the women and Mary the mother of Jesus, and with his brothers.

[15]In those days Peter stood up among the believers (a group numbering about a hundred and twenty)[16] and said, 'Brothers and sisters, the Scripture had to be fulfilled in which the Holy Spirit spoke long ago through David concerning Judas, who served as guide for those who arrested Jesus.[17] He was one of our number and shared in our ministry.'

[18](With the payment he received for his wickedness, Judas bought a field; there he fell headlong, his body burst open and all his intestines spilled out.[19] Everyone in Jerusalem heard about this, so they called that field in their language Akeldama, that is, Field of Blood.)

[20]'For,' said Peter, 'it is written in the Book of Psalms:

' "May his place be deserted;
let there be no one to dwell in it,"

and,

' "May another take his place of leadership."

[21]'Therefore it is necessary to choose one of the men who have been with us the whole time the Lord Jesus was living among us,[22] beginning from John's baptism to the time when Jesus was taken up from us. For one of these must become a witness with us of his resurrection.'

[23]So they nominated two men: Joseph called Barsabbas (also known as Justus) and Matthias.[24] Then they prayed, 'Lord, you know

APPENDIX: *Scripture passages for Meditation* 99

everyone's heart. Show us which of these two you have chosen[25] to take over this apostolic ministry, which Judas left to go where he belongs.'[26] Then they cast lots, and the lot fell to Matthias; so he was added to the eleven apostles.

John 15.1-11

[1]'I am the true vine, and my Father is the gardener.[2] He cuts off every branch in me that bears no fruit, while every branch that does bear fruit he prunes so that it will be even more fruitful.[3] You are already clean because of the word I have spoken to you.[4] Remain in me, as I also remain in you. No branch can bear fruit by itself; it must remain in the vine. Neither can you bear fruit unless you remain in me.

[5]'I am the vine; you are the branches. If you remain in me and I in you, you will bear much fruit; apart from me you can do nothing.[6] If you do not remain in me, you are like a branch that is thrown away and withers; such branches are picked up, thrown into the fire and burned.[7] If you remain in me and my words remain in you, ask whatever you wish, and it will be done for you.[8] This is to my Father's glory, that you bear much fruit, showing yourselves to be my disciples.

[9]'As the Father has loved me, so have I loved you. Now remain in my love.[10] If you keep my commands, you will remain in my love, just as I have kept my Father's commands and remain in his love.[11] I have told you this so that my joy may be in you and that your joy may be complete.'

John 16.5-15

Jesus said,[5] 'But now I am going to him who sent me. None of you asks me, "Where are you going?"[6] Rather, you are filled with grief because I have said these things.[7] But very truly I tell you, it is for your good that I am going away. Unless I go away, the Advocate will not come to you; but if I go, I will send him to you.[8] When he comes, he will prove the world to be in the wrong about sin and right-eousness and judgment:[9] about sin, because people do not believe in me;[10] about righteousness, because I am going to the Father, where you can see me no longer;[11] and about judgment, because the prince of this world now stands condemned.

[12]'I have much more to say to you, more than you can now bear.[13] But when he, the Spirit of truth, comes, he will guide you into all the truth. He will not speak on his own; he will speak only what he hears, and he will tell you what is yet to come.[14] He will glorify me because it is from me that he will receive what he will make known to you.[15] All that belongs to the Father is mine. That is why I said the Spirit will receive from me what he will make known to you.'

Easter Day   Coming home

Lamentations 3.22-28, Acts 20.26-32, John 17.11-end

Lamentations 3.22-28

[22]Because of the LORD's great love we are not consumed,
  for his compassions never fail.
[23]They are new every morning;
  great is your faithfulness.
[24]I say to myself, 'The LORD is my portion;
  therefore I will wait for him.'
[25]The LORD is good to those whose hope is in him,
  to the one who seeks him;
[26]it is good to wait quietly
  for the salvation of the LORD.
[27]It is good for a man to bear the yoke
  while he is young.
[28]Let him sit alone in silence,
  for the LORD has laid it on him.

Acts 20.26-32

[26]'Therefore, I declare to you today that I am innocent of the blood of any of you.[27] For I have not hesitated to proclaim to you the

whole will of God.[28] Keep watch over yourselves and all the flock of which the Holy Spirit has made you overseers. Be shepherds of the church of God, which he bought with his own blood.[29] I know that after I leave, savage wolves will come in among you and will not spare the flock.[30] Even from your own number men will arise and distort the truth in order to draw away disciples after them.[31] So be on your guard! Remember that for three years I never stopped warning each of you night and day with tears.

[32]'Now I commit you to God and to the word of his grace, which can build you up and give you an inheritance among all those who are sanctified.'

John 17.11-26

Jesus said,[11] 'I will remain in the world no longer, but they are still in the world, and I am coming to you. Holy Father, protect them by the power of your name, the name you gave me, so that they may be one as we are one.[12] While I was with them, I protected them and kept them safe by that name you gave me. None has been lost except the one doomed to destruction so that Scripture would be fulfilled.

[13]'I am coming to you now, but I say these things while I am still in the world, so that they may have the full measure of my joy within them.[14] I have given them your word and the world has hated them, for they are not of the world any more than I am of the world.[15] My prayer is not that you take them out of the world but that you protect them from the evil one.[16] They are not of the world, even as I am not of it.[17] Sanctify them by the truth; your word is truth.[18] As you sent me into the world, I have sent them into the world.[19] For them I sanctify myself, that they too may be truly sanctified.

[20]'My prayer is not for them alone. I pray also for those who will believe in me through their message,[21] that all of them may be one, Father, just as you are in me and I am in you. May they also be in us so that the world may believe that you have sent me.[22] I have given them the glory that you gave me, that they may be one as we are one –[23] I in them and you in me – so that they may be brought to

complete unity. Then the world will know that you sent me and have loved them even as you have loved me.

[24]'Father, I want those you have given me to be with me where I am, and to see my glory, the glory you have given me because you loved me before the creation of the world.

[25]'Righteous Father, though the world does not know you, I know you, and they know that you have sent me. [26] I have made you known to them, and will continue to make you known in order that the love you have for me may be in them and that I myself may be in them.'